Tiger's Heart

tiger's heart

BY KIT BRENNAN

Tiger's Heart
first published 1996 by
Scirocco Drama
An imprint of J. Gordon Shillingford Publishing Inc.
© 1993 Kit Brennan

Cover design by Terry Gallagher/Doowah Design
Author photo by Jonas Papaurelis
Printed and bound in Canada by Les Ateliers Graphiques Marc Veilleux

Published with the generous assistance of The Canada Council.

All rights reserved. No part of this book may be reproduced, for any reason, by any means, without the permission of the publisher. This play is fully protected under the copyright laws of Canada and all other countries of the Copyright Union and is subject to royalty. Changes to the text are expressly forbidden without written consent of the author. Rights to produce, film, record in whole or in part, in any medium or in any language, by any group amateur or professional, are retained by the author.
Production inquiries should be addressed to:
Donna Wong-Juliani
P.O. Box 2050, M.P.O.
Vancouver, BC V6B 3R6

Canadian Cataloguing in Publication Data

Brennan, Kit, 1957-
    Tiger's heart

A play.
ISBN 1-896239-13-7

    I. Title.
PS8553.R3843T53 1996   C812'.54   C96-900132-0
PR9199.3.B69158T53 1996

For Jan Selman, a great enabler

Acknowledgements

I would like to acknowledge the assistance of Great Canadian Theatre Company, the 1993 Banff Centre for the Arts Playwrights' Colony, Theatre B.C., the Department of Drama at the University of Alberta, the Department of Theatre and Film Studies at the University of British Columbia, Workshop West Theatre, and the Ontario Arts Council. Also the Alberta Heritage Scholarship Fund, whose Ralph Steinhauer Award gave me time to write and rewrite the early drafts. Many thanks to Jan Selman, Arthur Milner, Colin Taylor, David Barnett and, always, Andrew Willmer.

Production History

Tiger's Heart was premiered by Great Canadian Theatre Company in Ottawa, Canada, in February, 1995, with the following cast:

DR. JAMES BARRY .... Beverley Wolfe
LORD CHARLES SOMERSET .... David Schurmann
DANTZEN/TRACKER .... Mxolisi Welcome Ngozi
CAPTAIN JOSIAH CLOETE .... John Koensgen
MAGGIE, PROSTITUTE,
LADY SOMERSET, GEORGIANA .... Diana Fajrajsl

Directed by Colin Taylor
Costume design by Thea Yeatman
Lighting design by Martin J. Conboy
Lighting assistant: Jon Alexander
Sound design by Ian Tamblyn
Set design by Art Penson
Stage Manager: Wendy Rockburn

Tiger's Heart received its second production at the Frederic Wood Theatre in Vancouver, Canada, as part of the *1996 Women in View Festival* in January, 1996, with the following cast:

DR. JAMES BARRY	Sophie Yendole
LORD CHARLES SOMERSET	John Juliani
DANTZEN/TRACKER	Danny Waugh
CAPTAIN JOSIAH CLOETE	Cameron Cronin
PROSTITUTE	Sarah Eeckhout
MAGGIE	Krista Endrizzi
LADY SOMERSET	Sharon Feder
AUCTIONEER	David Pauls
GEORGIANA	Jacqueline Prince
KRAMER	Rob Stover
WARDEN	Bryn Williams
SECOND	Peter Wilson
AFRICAN DANCER	Raugauhaan Yu
ENVIRONS (CHORUS)	Marya Delver, Sarah Eeckhout, Sharon Feder, David Pauls, Jacqueline Prince, Rob Stover, Bryn Williams, Peter Wilson, Raugauhaan Yu

Directed by Jan Selman
Set, masks, and costume design by Norma Rodgers
Lighting design by Robert Gardiner
Choreography by Cathy Burnett
Sound design/composition by Greg Ray
Stage Manager: Meaghan Benmore

Casting Requirements

Tiger's Heart may be performed with a cast as few as five, and as many as twelve, depending upon artistic conception and resources. The role breakdowns for a cast of five are as follows:

Women:
1. DR. JAMES BARRY.
2. MAGGIE, the PROSTITUTE, LADY SOMERSET, and GEORGIANA.

Men:
1. DANTZEN, and the TRACKER (GALAWA, DANTZEN's son).
2. LORD CHARLES SOMERSET, and AUCTIONEER, SECOND.
3. CAPTAIN JOSIAH CLOETE, and WARDEN.

With a slightly larger cast, a breakdown suggestion might be to allow each of the lead characters not to double, but to maintain some doubling of minor roles. With a full-sized cast, as many as ten to twelve actors may be easily accommodated.

If you intend to expand the cast size, see notes on the next page.

Notes for a Larger Cast

DANTZEN and GALAWA (TRACKER): This is the most clearly unified doubling indicated for a cast of five; the TRACKER transforms into his father during the course of the "hunt", and then returns into the present to confront the elderly BARRY. However, this doubling, also, could be cast with two actors. In that case, other choices must be made for scene segues than those indicated in the text.

The WOMEN: One actor can easily play all of the women characters, and there is thematic interest in this doubling: they are all creatures without power—except perhaps LADY MARY, whose near death labour and strength to recover signals the beginnings of a new power in her. Nevertheless, more than one actor playing these parts frees up MAGGIE, enhances the ball scene, and provides contrast.

MAGGIE: There are other places where MAGGIE could appear as a ghost-like figure when she is spoken of, either in the foreground (weaving through the action, seen by no one but BARRY) or well in the background. Examples of possible foregrounding are in Scene 11 (Nightmare) and of backgrounding, Scene 13 (Sister), as BARRY relives the memory of finding her sister on a morgue slab.

Scene 2 (The Ball): There are obvious possibilities here for other women to be gathering and whispering and longing to dance. Should this be the case, a fuller sense of the "ball" in progress may be accomplished. Barry would flirt with them gallantly. All of the women should wear various prey masks (antelope, eland, etc.).
—in the scene:
SOMERSET: "Tonight you shall be meeting our colony's young belles."
—replace with "What do you think of our young belles?"

Notes on Staging

The play opens and closes in Cape Town, South Africa, in 1850; the body of the play takes place in Cape Town from 1820-1822.

The first scene, The Two-Faced, introduces the characters in a dreamlike way, which the play then unravels. The final scene returns us to that place and those images, with the meeting of BARRY and GALAWA.

The play seems to work best when offered at a rapid pace. Fluidity between scenes is crucial. At pace, the first act plays around 65 minutes. The play is a drama, yet there is intentional humour, and it is important to have that relief.

For British history, this is an era of repressed physicality, the raging greed of colonization. These are animals in civilized clothing. Sex, and ambition, and what desire for those things can do. Public and private, masks are pervasive.

The actor playing BARRY needs to find the *male* side of the character, for BARRY's disguise is authentic, having by now lived the lie for ten years.

Historically, SOMERSET is 45 years of age in 1820, CLOETE is 35, BARRY, 24. However, the important point is that BARRY is relatively new at the game, while SOMERSET is at the height of his power and charisma.

MAGGIE is BARRY's dead sister. During the first production, we found it effective to have her violent death manifested by a trail of blood. Her nightmare pattern is haunting, speechless. She moves in and through dream and waking reality.

The TRACKER's place: In different productions, this has been variously interpreted by an upper level, or by an actual tree which he climbs and thus is above, observing.

Pronounciations

GEORGIANA is pronounced "Georg-ee-*en*-a". CLOETE's name is pronounced by the British "Kloo-tee", by himself and other Dutch "Kluoo-tugh". The Hemel and Aarde (Heaven and Earth) leper colony is pronounced "H-Yem-el and Ar-duh", meneer is "men-*ear*", kaffir is "kaff-ear" (an extremely negative modern connotation, correct for the period). "Yirra" is an Afrikaans expletive pronounced "H-Yirra" (the real word is written "Here")—the meaning is roughly "good god". "Blerry" means bloody—pronounced "blairy". DANTZEN's real name (Maqoma) is Xhosa, the "q" with the click, sometimes written as "!"—"Ma!qoma". GALAWA is pronounced "Gah-*lah*-wa". Sibongele is "Si-*bong*-gel-ay" ("gel" with a hard "g"). Mlungu ("m-loong-goo") means "white man". The lines in Xhosa should be delivered in Xhosa if at all possible, in which case the English translation of the line will *not* be said, except where noted..

A slash (/) indicates where voices overlap, the overlap coinciding with the line *below*.

Foreword

Tiger's Heart is based on the true story of Dr. James Barry, but it does not purport to be an entirely historical portrayal of this fascinating person.

The real Dr. Barry lived from approximately 1795-1865. Born in Ireland of a poor family, Barry attended university in Edinburgh, and wrote a doctoral thesis on Hernia of the Groin. Shortly thereafter, Barry joined the army and was posted to Cape Town. Throughout a long career, the doctor's reforms and humanitarian measures were far ahead of their time, and had far-reaching consequences. Research into hygiene, and tireless campaigning for, in Barry's words, "the unfortunates of every system—women, blacks, and maniacs", won better conditions for many of the downtrodden in British colonial outposts worldwide. Dr. Barry moved slowly but contentiously up through the ranks of the Army Medical Department, finally attaining the position of Inspector General of Hospitals. Near the end of forty-five years of active service in far-flung tropical colonies from St. Helena to Trinidad, Barry was posted to Montreal, Canada, and was a member of the St. James Club there. The cold did not agree with the doctor, however, and after two years, Barry returned to England suffering from pneumonia and bronchitis, and from thence to retirement, warmer climates, and obscurity—until death, in London in 1865, catapulted Barry back into the public arena.

A charwoman paid to lay out the body rushed around to the Army Medical Department in London declaiming vehemently that Barry was a woman, and "moreover, a woman who has borne a child!" The charwoman wished to be paid for keeping this secret. Letters flew back and forth between colleagues and doctors from Montreal to London to Trinidad—how could this be true of one of their senior medical officers? A scandal, to be hushed up at all costs. Barry's good name and reforms, as well as her body, were buried as deep as the Department could dig them.

Apocryphal accounts of the nature of the doctor's person, however, began to surface several years later in *The Lancet* and in Charles Dicken's magazine *All the Year Round*. One Colonel Rogers, who claimed to have known Barry, wrote a romantic novel called "A Modern Sphinx" (1881), based on his speculations. Another small flurry of letters in *The Lancet* in 1895 once again revived interest, partly spurred by Rogers, who hoped to engender another printing of his book. As human nature will have it, other now elderly subscribers appeared who "knew" all along that Barry had been a woman.

Popular speculations of the *reason* for Barry's life-long masquerade have followed one of several paths: a) the tragic: she was an ugly woman and unlucky in love; b) the romantic: she was jilted by an army doctor whom she had followed into the army; or c) the semi-liberated: she followed the advice of high-powered male patrons who saw she had a good brain and who bravely devised a way for her to put her brain to use. None of these theories take into account the good brain which can think for itself and decide that the life of poverty and enslavement to which a woman was fated in her circumstances, class, and century was simply not good enough, and that a life in perpetual disguise, freely chosen, could be more rewarding than one endured in virtual female enslavement in Victorian Britain. I was much less interested in the "why" of Barry's decision—this seemed to me self evident—than in the "how"; *how* did she do it, and so brilliantly?

Tiger's Heart began as a feature-length screenplay, with a different title, in 1992. As I finished, I began to feel it might be exciting and challenging to take this large a story and force it into the straightjacket of the theatre. Confinement might make for a passionate, cut-to-the-chase theatrical event. I decided to focus upon the years in Cape Town, when Barry was in her twenties, young and idealistic and ambitious, and already secure in her disguise. Cape Town seemed a catalyst for many things. The British colony in South Africa was then very new, the lust and greed of colonization strong. Slavery was still very much a part of the fabric of that society. Abolition did not happen until twenty-five years later—which prompted my addition of Galawa, Dantzen's son, come back to reclaim knowledge of his father and his father's death. It became a story of a hunt across time and continents.

Most of the details of Barry's life and work during the period reflected in the play are accurate, but I have taken liberties with history. The largest liberties are outlined here.

Although Captain Cloete *did* pull Barry's nose, and they *did* fight a duel, no evidence suggests that they were in fact duelling for Lord Charles Somerset's favour. Barry was indeed the first white doctor on the African continent ever to perform an operation for caesarian section and save the life of both woman and child (there was no anaesthetic at this time); however, the child was not in fact born of Lady Mary Somerset but of the wife of one Thomas Munnik, a tobacco merchant, whose family was so grateful to Dr. Barry that for over one hundred years, each first-born male descendant has been christened James Barry Munnik. Lord Charles Somerset *was* taken to task for promoting and favouring the young doctor, and later reprimanded for abuse of funds and overtaxation of the fledgling colony. He was, fact, removed from his position as Governor, and requested to return to England, but his Aide de Camp Captain Josiah Cloete did not engineer this downfall. Barry's real name *may* have been Marion, and she *may* have had a sister, but Maggie is my own invention, fleshing out the image of what a poor woman could expect from a life unprotected, of Barry's fear of ever being forced to "go back", and of her drive to help people without power. Barry may have had a child (the charwoman asserted that the body bore the stretch marks of childbirth when young), but no one knows what became of the child if there was one, nor who may have fathered it. Although Barry did keep a servant, and some accounts name that servant Dantzen, there is no evidence that the two were ever more than master and slave. Their relationship and eventual love is a bold and outrageous assertion on my part, as historians have not hesitated to tell me, but it is crucial to my interpretation of Barry's character and spirit, and to the tragedy of her ambition, where scoring points becomes—even for one satisfying moment—more important than another human being whom she loves.

Articles still appear from time to time debating Barry's gender. Many seem to me to seek to disparage Barry's accomplishments and aplomb. There are those who insist that Barry was a man, although an effeminate one—or perhaps a hermaphrodite—or perhaps a man whose genitalia never descended properly—etc. etc. Other articles claim Barry's eccentric love for animals and hot-tempered irrationality point to a lonely, aging, little woman. "Lonely" certainly—how did she manage this life-long secret, hugged forever in silence? This became a major jumping-off point for me—surely there must have been *someone*?

Above and beyond the fascination with Barry's gender (which inevitably superceded the doctor's medical achievements), I prefer to see Barry as a strong-minded individual who made a tough choice in a tough world, saw the adventure through to its end, and paid the price, with fortitude at the very least. Anything less, Barry does not deserve. And the truth—she did not want us to know.

For further information about Dr. James Barry, I recommend the final chapter in *Eminent Victorian Women* by Elizabeth Longford (Weidenfeld and Nicolson, London, 1981), and the well-researched *The Perfect Gentleman* by June Rose (Hutchinson & Co (Publishers) Ltd., London, 1977).

Kit Brennan
January 1996

"O tiger's heart, wrapped in a woman's hide."
—*Henry VI*, Part III

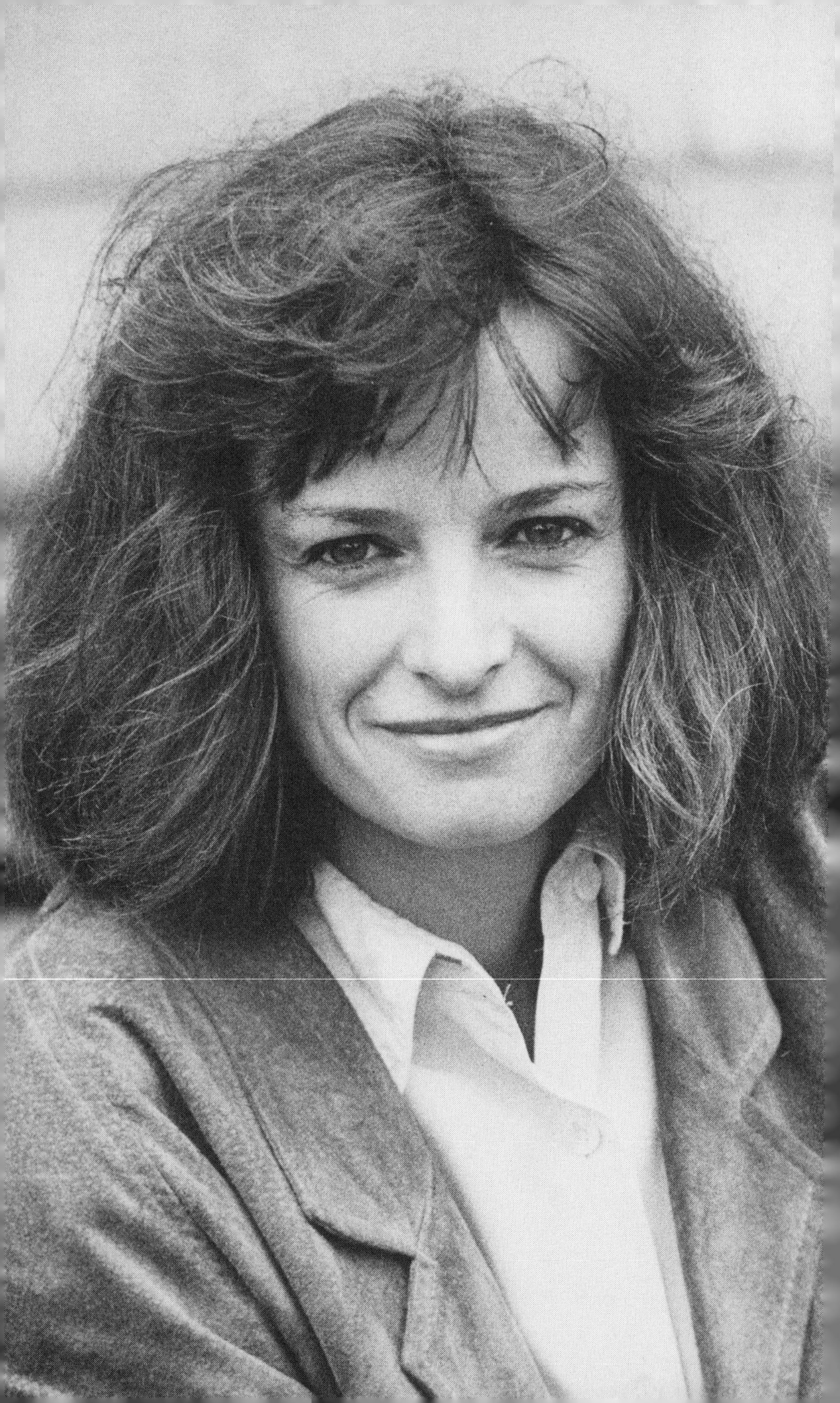

Kit Brennan

Kit Brennan was born in Vancouver and grew up in Kingston, Ontario. She currently lives in Montreal where she is a faculty member of the Theatre Department at Concordia University. Her other plays include *Spring Planting* (Winner of the Saskatchewan Writer's Guild 1993 Literary Award) and *Magpie* (Winner of the 1992 Grain Drama Award).

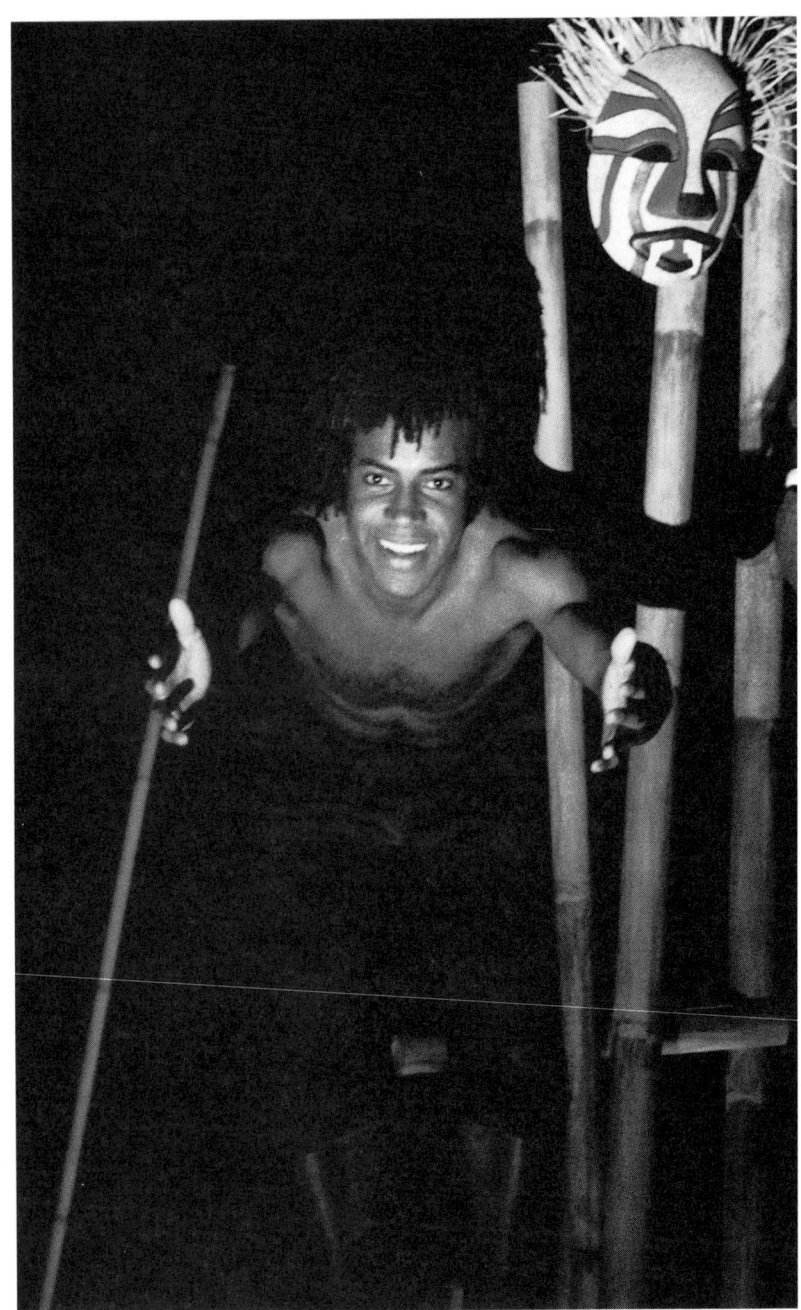

The Tracker

Act I

Scene One The Two-Faced

(1850. Cape Town, South Africa. Behind, three figures can be barely seen: a woman, binding her breasts, then dressing in military pants, shirt, and jacket. A man with a gun, wearing a grinning mask. A ghost-like female figure. In the foreground, the TRACKER, crouching, is a black man in his thirties.)

TRACKER: There's a dream in my head. My feet in this earth. A scent, very faint, coming up from this ground.

I am a tracker. I have travelled far. Returned to this place, where it all began. Thirty years past, my father, my mother—ripped apart, sold at auction. Soon after, she died. Sold again, I grew to manhood, in India, in Nepal, tracking tigers for the maharajah. But my dreams always here, in Africa, with my father.

(He picks up the mask of an impassive face.)

When I was a boy, in the grasses, we'd go walking. "Fear the old ones, the man-eaters" he told me, my father. "They attack from behind, won't look prey in the eye. That is why we wear these. We are—

(Puts the mask on the back of his head.)

—two-faced. Invulnerable." Then he'd laugh. "Come on now, Galawa." I was small, afraid. It can't be so simple, I'd think, and hang back. When we enter their territory, we take what comes.

(The TRACKER senses the presence of the others. Dappled light where jungle meets plain. The man, SOMERSET, begins to stalk. The ghost figure, MAGGIE, walks.)

They passed this way, long ago. Dreams and dark deeds, father.

(SOMERSET cautiously turns the mask to the back of his head; then turns and fires. A big cat roar.)

In every hunting, there is a lust.

(SOMERSET and MAGGIE exit. BARRY, fully dressed, enters the world evoked by the TRACKER and looks around.)

BARRY: Africa's far. Not far enough.

(BARRY exits. The TRACKER reveals the Cape Town setting.)

TRACKER: I will know the truth of my father. Somewhere in the dark, rippled border of forest and plain, light and shadow, good and evil—who is eating, who is eaten? I am here, they are here, the traces of their passing. I slip into the past like a second skin, following the shadow of a dream.

(The TRACKER puts on his impassive mask, enters scene as servant.)

Dr. James Barry

The Ball

Photo by Andrée Lanthier

Scene Two The Ball

(1820. Sound of musicians, tuning up. Lord Charles SOMERSET, Governor of Cape Town, with a lion mask. CAPTAIN JOSIAH CLOETE, SOMERSET's Aide de Camp, big and handsome, with a red dog, or hyena, mask.)

CLOETE: He's a dandy, Lord Somerset. Bullheaded in the wards.

SOMERSET: The survival rate of patients has increased, I am told.

CLOETE: And the cost of supplies has tripled. He's put a ban on salt beef, says it's bad for one!

SOMERSET: Does he? You eat my share then, Cloete.

CLOETE: Governor, you must stop him. He's begun to *treat* the kaffirs in his clinic—asking *them* to tell him what's wrong.

SOMERSET: And where are the kaffirs' mistresses?

CLOETE: Standing by, scandalized and titillated, both. A doctor, conversing with a Bantu, when a Christian is before him? Well, you can imagine.

SOMERSET: Mm.

CLOETE: Young pups from England.

(CLOETE sees BARRY, just entering, in a leopard mask.)

There he is now.

SOMERSET: He's unfashionably early.

CLOETE: Have to find him a wife. He's been causing a few hearts to flutter; our newest bachelor.

SOMERSET: Ha! you're jealous. Poaching on your preserve.

CLOETE: Concerned for the ladies, that's all.

SOMERSET: Bring me the puppy.

(CLOETE clicks his heels, bows, approaches BARRY.)

CLOETE: The Governor wishes a word.

(BARRY returns with CLOETE, bows.)

SOMERSET: Dr. Barry. Welcome to Government House.

BARRY: An honour, Your Excellency.

SOMERSET: You came well recommended, Lord Buchan and so on. But young, very green, hm? You must purchase a domestic; makes life bearable at the Cape. Purchase several. And you needn't feel guilty, all this liberal hogwash. No gentleman here is without one.

BARRY: I like my privacy.

CLOETE: If you keep no servant, people will talk, they will say you are peculiar.

BARRY: I *am* peculiar, Captain.

SOMERSET: Smooth your hackles, gentlemen. This is a social, not a combative, event. A night for our decorative young ladies to shine.

(GEORGIANA enters, in an antelope mask, excited.)

CLOETE: Miss Georgiana. May I...?

SOMERSET: Not yet, Cloete.

(CLOETE bows and retreats to the windows.)

What are our lazy houseboys up to, leaving me high and dry. Boy!

(The masked servant approaches with drinks. CLOETE moves to GEORGIANA, who ignores him.)

You a rebel, Barry? Find our old-fashioned notions and habits galling?

BARRY: Not at all, Your Lordship.

SOMERSET: Of course, there is no slavery as such in Cape Town proper. Here, there is kindness and employment.

BARRY: In England we're told—

SOMERSET: One must prepare a people for freedom, Barry, or they will not be ready for it when it comes. Well, leave that. Tonight you shall be meeting our colony's young belles. Not a mind between them, but pretty to look at for all that.

BARRY: I am—a solitary sort, Your Lordship. Except in a crowd. There I do my best.

SOMERSET: Good. Good. We could do with less tomcatting among our officers. Set an example. Very good.

(CLOETE tries to engage GEORGIANA.)

CLOETE: May I have this...?

GEORGIANA: No.

(GEORGIANA flounces away; CLOETE gets himself a drink.)

SOMERSET: I need your advice. Professionally. Ticklish sort of health I enjoy. Take the waters, that sort of thing, but I—

(GEORGIANA joins them.)

GEORGIANA: Is Papa outlining his various ailments?

SOMERSET: Run along, Georgiana.

GEORGIANA: You're the new doctor, aren't you?

(BARRY kisses her hand.)

Charmed.

(She goes. CLOETE is badly ruffled, SOMERSET amused.)

SOMERSET: A doctor's bedside manner can become addictive here. I'd be careful.

(They laugh.)

I am a widower. For a—number of years. Two daughters, no sons. Came for the hunting, stayed to be Governor. But the adventure, that's what drew me. An undiscovered country. Not many of those left. Each one is a possibility, hm?—each one might be paradise. If you can find it, the heart of it; claim it for your own.

BARRY: Yes.

SOMERSET: Feel the same? Thought you might. You may find, over time, that the—climate—does not fundamentally agree. If you're at all like me. I've found I need...other things.

BARRY: Oh really? Such as?

SOMERSET: Sturm und drang. Storms!

BARRY: I...don't understand.

SOMERSET: Oppressive days and nights, and yet—the promise of impending—excitement. Not this everlasting heat, without relief....Do you follow me?

BARRY: We could do with a night breeze, Your Lordship. It feels...close. Very. Close.

(BARRY sees a white tiger hide, displayed.)

Where did you get this miraculous skin?

SOMERSET: Hunting in India. Guest of the maharajah. Very exciting. Very bloodthirsty. Beautiful animal.

BARRY: Indeed. I've never seen such a creature.

SOMERSET: Neither had I. Rare. Very...exotic. Blue eyes, blue gems—impossible to capture.

(BARRY strokes the hide, SOMERSET watches him)

SOMERSET: Much like yours. Dr. Barry. That startling blue.

BARRY: ...Perhaps we should—

SOMERSET: Be aware, hm? There are scavengers. Seek protection.

(CLOETE approaches. The musicians have begun to play a waltz.)

SOMERSET: —And good doctoring, above all! My own man Struwig's a quack, I'm sure of it. We'll talk again. My daughter, Georgiana—she's longing to dance.

BARRY: You don't object?

(BARRY goes to GEORGIANA, putting on his mask.)

CLOETE: Your Lordship, I—!

SOMERSET: Let her dance with the new man. She's had enough of you, Cloete. Haven't we all.

(BARRY and GEORGIANA dance. BARRY is very good.)

CLOETE: What is it, Governor? You're—

SOMERSET: Puzzled. Just...puzzled, old friend.

BARRY: Too fast, Miss Georgiana?

GEORGIANA: Oh no, it is lovely! Can we go faster?

BARRY: We can try.

(GEORGIANA laughs in delight.)

CLOETE: Pocket-sized little—

SOMERSET: I like him! New blood to keep us on our toes.

(BARRY looks over, and SOMERSET raises his glass. Hunters and hunted. The ball disperses, the TRACKER removes his mask. He has located the main players; he becomes DANTZEN.)

30   Tiger's Heart

Scene Three   The Auction

(Stable; the dregs of an auction.)

CLOETE: Not much here. I was hoping to find a new mare, but it seems they're all taken. Just the nags left. What about you, Barry? What's your fancy?

BARRY: Along for the ride, Captain. Not in the market for horseflesh today.

CLOETE: They're all too big. You'd need a pony.

BARRY: I can throw my leg over the best of them.

CLOETE: Oh I know it. I'm sure of it. Quite the ladykiller, ja?

(BARRY sees DANTZEN crouched in a corner.)

BARRY: Wait a moment. *(To DANTZEN.)* What are you doing there? Are you hurt?

DANTZEN: ...No sir.

CLOETE: Oh come away. You're not in the clinic now.

(Auctioneer bustles back.)

AUCTIONEER: What can I do for you gentlem—You there, get up. On your feet. Up!

BARRY: Do you know this boy?

AUCTIONEER: Property of the deceased. Couldn't sell him today. Wouldn't stand so they could see him.

BARRY: I think he's hurt.

AUCTIONEER: I'll give him hurt. Get along there, now!

BARRY: I won't harm you. Ah, look at these contusions, open welts. What's happened to you?

CLOETE: Lazy's my bet.

BARRY: What will you do with him?

AUCTIONEER: Vineyards. Somewhere. He's costing me.

BARRY: How much?

AUCTIONEER: You want him?

CLOETE: Don't be foolish, Barry, he's obviously unskilled. And you haven't the slightest idea about kaffirs.

BARRY: Yes. Yes I do want him.

AUCTIONEER: Well then! He's been apprenticing as interior domestic, but seeing he's somewhat—

BARRY: What, what? What figure, man?

AUCTIONEER: One hundred fifty pounds sterling. The equivalent in rix dollars. Doctor.

BARRY: I understand the currency. Here is the address, mark it to my attention: Dr. James Barry. Now leave us, yes?

(He does.)

The vineyards are brutal. He'd die in a month, with these wounds.

CLOETE: Ja, sure. Welcome to Cape Town, Barry.

(CLOETE smiles, exits. BARRY and DANTZEN are wary of each other.)

BARRY: What's your name?

DANTZEN: Dantzen. Sir.

BARRY: I'll tell you a secret: I'm as scared as you are.

DANTZEN: ...You paid too much. He cheated you, sir.

(Pause.)

BARRY: Let's get you home.

Scene Four Prostitute

(Prison Hospital. A PROSTITUTE, bruised, with a dirty face, is trying to tie a red velvet ribbon around her throat.)

PROSTITUTE: Ach, you stupid thing then. Shakin', that's what it is. Stupid thing.

(BARRY enters, with doctor's bag.)

BARRY: Don't be frightened, I won't hurt you.

PROSTITUTE: Makes a change.

BARRY: Would you sit. What's your name?

PROSTITUTE: What's it to you....Betty. Betts. Lizabett once. What you like. 'Elp us out, love?

BARRY: *(Noticing mark on her neck, ties ribbon.)* What's the ribbon for?

PROSTITUTE: Fashion, what'd you think.

BARRY: Tell me about yourself.

PROSTITUTE: You're tickling.

BARRY: Sorry.

PROSTITUTE: 'Salright. Born in England, just like you.

BARRY: *(Examining PROSTITUTE's chest and back.)* Ireland.

PROSTITUTE: Paddy then? Oo! Come here with me husband, three year ago. The Royal East India; powerful company, we had it all. Then, the men upped, new posting. Left us, wives and so on. No money, couldn't get home. What else could we do. Give us a bit of love then?

> (Places BARRY's hand on her breast. He doesn't remove it.)
>
> You're a gentleman, not like some. I miss their touch. Mm, you like that.
>
> (Moves BARRY's hand to her throat, to the gash of ribbon.)
>
> At your mercy, darlin'. What's the matter then? You look kind of queer.
>
> (BARRY moves away.)

BARRY: You're very ill.

PROSTITUTE: Don't have to tell me, I know.

BARRY: You have syphilis, secondary rashes. Know what that means?

PROSTITUTE: Need more than a bit o' velvet soon.

BARRY: You'll spread the disease.

PROSTITUTE: Serve them right, filthy buggers. They've been grabbing it for free in here.

BARRY: Who has?

PROSTITUTE: The men who tend us. Ah what do I care, I'm as good as dead. Twenty-six. Hard to believe, eh?

BARRY: This ointment might help. That will be all.

PROSTITUTE: You're afraid of me.

BARRY: Don't be cheeky.

PROSTITUTE: Scared of the pox then? You're hungry for skin though. Wear a tickler, you'll be safe—I'll take care of you.

BARRY: I'll be back in a few days.

PROSTITUTE: For you, it's free.

BARRY: Be quiet.

PROSTITUTE: You could have your pick, I swear, any woman in the

	Cape. Something about you. You're small, but handsome. I could please you. Bit o' rough.
BARRY:	Listen to me. I'll do my best for you. But do not, I tell you, do not cajole me with your body. I am not moved by it. I am moved by your plight.
PROSTITUTE:	Why d'you care then, eh?
BARRY:	You remind me of…someone.

(BARRY exits.)

PROSTITUTE:	You're lyin' about my body. I could feel you.

Scene Five To Learn

(BARRY's rooms. DANTZEN, with book. BARRY enters.)

BARRY: Don't get up. Yes, it's all right.

DANTZEN: I'll start with your jacket.

BARRY: Leave it for the morning. These interest you? You have reading?

DANTZEN: No sir.

BARRY: You have some, I'll warrant, yes? How?

DANTZEN: ...The children of the master. Loved learning. Loved teaching. I amused them.

BARRY: I see. I was lucky, a rich patron—believed in my mind, took an interest. As I do in you. How can I help you further your interest?

DANTZEN: May I go now.

BARRY: I make you that unhappy. I hoped... *(Beat.)* You can go.

DANTZEN: For those children, it was a game. But not for me. I remind you: it is against the law, meneer doctor.

BARRY: And you are afraid.

DANTZEN: Yes. Sir.

BARRY: I was afraid. But now: I don't allow it—not in myself, not in you. O brave new world, Dantzen. That's Shakespeare—best teacher, truest insights.

DANTZEN: I have my own teachers.

BARRY: Ah. I know what you're thinking: that this is a white man's game—that I'll trick you somehow, trap you.

DANTZEN: That's not what I'm thinking.

BARRY: Look here, I don't believe in master and servant. I've hired you, to do a job—that's how I look at it.

DANTZEN: You can look at it as you wish, sir, but in the law you own me, and in the law, your laws, these lines in these books are not to be learned by me. I don't want them.

BARRY: This is absurd. I want to *save* you, Dantzen. That's why I bought you, in that stable, and why I am taking such trouble over you! You'd think you'd be grateful!

DANTZEN: Were you grateful? ...Forgive me, meneer.

BARRY: No. Say what you were going to say, you've gone this far. Say it.

DANTZEN: Were you grateful, to your patron? To your rich man? Or were you thinking your own thoughts.

BARRY: Now there's a question. *(Beat.)* I want you to help me. In the clinic, on my rounds. I think it will be good for both of us, yes?

(Holds out book.)

Come on now. This is the best thing I can give you, Dantzen, the very best. Knowledge is power.

DANTZEN: Knowledge will kill me.

BARRY: Practice your reading.

(After a moment, DANTZEN takes the book.)

Good man.

DANTZEN: No. Good servant.

Scene Six Dreams

(Darkness. BARRY is dreaming. DANTZEN lights a lamp, crosses to listen outside BARRY's bedchamber. MAGGIE moves through the bedroom, blood at her throat and trailing.)

BARRY: Maggie? Maggie, don't go down there. Please. No. Maggie!

(BARRY wakes with a start as MAGGIE disappears. BARRY cries; loud, wrenching sobs which she tries but fails to muffle. DANTZEN retreats with the lantern.)

Scene Seven Unfortunates of Every System

(SOMERSET's room of business.)

SOMERSET: And he is...?

CLOETE: Difficult to drag away. He'd prefer to gaze at blisters and boils on black skins than obey the summons of his superiors.

(BARRY bursts in without knocking.)

BARRY: Your Lordship, forgive me. An insurmountable obstacle, a matter of—what did you call it, Cloete?—protocol.

SOMERSET: Ah! The Captain's favourite english word.

BARRY: Everywhere I turn I—I did not expect to be thwarted at every step by my own administration.

SOMERSET: You are one member of a large organization now, not the star pupil of a London anatomist. Your bodies are live, not dead, which is also an inconvenience.

BARRY: I intend to hire a respectable female to tend the women in the prison hospital. They are being abused by the male orderlies.

CLOETE: I've told him, any woman who'd consent to such a job is a drunkard. It's in your best interests—

BARRY: To abuse them myself? They are being raped, Cloete, is that plain english for you?

CLOETE: They are prostitutes!

BARRY: They are—aah! Governor?

(Both turn to him. He keeps them waiting.)

SOMERSET: Cloete, give him his head on this one, I can't understand why you came to me.

BARRY: There! Thank you, Your Lordship. I felt sure you would see clearly.

SOMERSET: Good work, Barry.

(SOMERSET smiles, begins to write again.)

BARRY: Secondly—

SOMERSET: One thing at a time, doctor. Another day, another day.

(CLOETE smirks. BARRY bows.)

CLOETE: Before you go. A letter. Marked Personal.

BARRY: How did it come to you?

CLOETE: A mistake. Incorrect filing.

BARRY: The seal is broken.

CLOETE: It was in my correspondence, I did not check the name.

BARRY: Have you read it?

CLOETE: No.

BARRY: You saw my name on the inside, is that it?

CLOETE: ...Yes.

BARRY: Ah.

CLOETE: Barry—

BARRY: Captain?

CLOETE: Good day.

BARRY: *(Bows)* Your Lordship.

(BARRY exits.)

SOMERSET: Anything I should know.

CLOETE: From his mother. Asking for money.

SOMERSET: Excellent. Keep him strapped; good for a young man's morale. About this other. You could simply ensure that all the females interviewed are unacceptable.

CLOETE: If—then why—

SOMERSET: I couldn't disappoint him. He's so keen! As you were once.

CLOETE: Long ago.

SOMERSET: Very long ago. Yes.

Scene Eight The Prison Hospital

(BARRY and DANTZEN enter a dirty room, DANTZEN with BARRY's medical bag.)

BARRY: The entire prison's a disgrace. Feces and food scraps, flies and rats!

WARDEN: *(off)* Get along there, you!

(The PROSTITUTE enters.)

BARRY: Sit here, Lizabett. Why are you whimpering?

PROSTITUTE: Me arm.

BARRY: How long have you been like this?

PROSTITUTE: Five days.

(The WARDEN enters.)

BARRY: What happened to you?

WARDEN: She fell down and...

BARRY: I didn't ask you. *(To PROSTITUTE.)* Come. You can tell me.

(The PROSTITUTE shakes her head.)

Someone broke it for you, yes?

(After a moment, she nods. BARRY glares at the WARDEN.)

I report fully to the Governor, and have no doubt that he will rectify this situation, and your authority, immediately! How much are you paid?

WARDEN: I...

BARRY: Too much! A week to reduce this slovenliness, or we reduce your wages by fifty percent. I want it spotless.

WARDEN: Under whose authority—

BARRY: Easier to clean it up, Warden. *(To PROSTITUTE.)* This is mending badly. I'll have to break it again and reset it, or your arm will stiffen in its present position and become useless. *(To WARDEN.)* Clear out, you. I don't want your carrion face feeding on her pain.

(The WARDEN goes.)

You have new sores. Don't you? Let me see.

PROSTITUTE: Help me, doctor.

BARRY: I will.

PROSTITUTE: Can't stand pain, see.

BARRY: Dear Lord...let me see this.

PROSTITUTE: There's something else, in't there? Something more, I know it.

BARRY: You shouldn't be here, you should be in the Hemel and Aarde colony. You have leprosy.

PROSTITUTE: Leprosy? Oh come on, lovey, forget the arm and break my little neck.

BARRY: Please stop that.

PROSTITUTE: You wouldn't help me, would you, nor your handsome boy there. One little snap, boy, do his dirty work, that's what they keep us for—I am dying!

BARRY: Shh now.

PROSTITUTE: I wish I were dead!

BARRY: Dantzen, help me here. You'll do yourself an injury. You are important to me—look at me—you resemble my sister, my sister that died. She was very much...like you. I intend to save you. You're under my special charge.

PROSTITUTE: In all pity, doctor.

BARRY: Be brave, sweetheart, soon be over. I will count to three. Are you ready? One. Two. Three.

(Lights down as the PROSTITUTE screams.)

Scene Nine To Learn II

(Outside. BARRY, leaning against a wall, retching.)

DANTZEN: She is right.

BARRY: Rotting away. Poor creature.

DANTZEN: You don't do what she needs. Instead, you break her arm.

BARRY: I'm a doctor! There may be a cure.

DANTZEN: It is another cruelty.

BARRY: How dare you judge me. How dare you, hey?

DANTZEN: She will suffer, and she will die in agony, six months, one year, from now. This also is slavery.

BARRY: You are telling me to kill another human being?

DANTZEN: I am reminding you of compassion! I am not a stone. I cannot stay a stone, following at your heels.

BARRY: As you're fond of reminding me, you are *paid* to follow, so do so, and be quiet! *(Wipes mouth.)* Jesus, god. What is happening to me? Dantzen, what are you telling me.

DANTZEN: I am telling you nothing.

BARRY: Help me. Come on, help me. This hatred, I can't bear it. We should talk to each other—we have no one else.

DANTZEN: You are wrong! I have a wife! A little boy!

BARRY: Why didn't you say so, I—

DANTZEN: I don't know where they are!

(Pause.)

BARRY: Tell me what happened.

DANTZEN: Why should I trust you.

BARRY: I...don't know.

DANTZEN: I see my boy in that woman's eyes. Is that not enough?

(Pause.)

BARRY: You challenge me. Every day. Most men wouldn't stand for it.

DANTZEN: I believe you are not most men. How much courage, I want to know. How much do you have?

Scene Ten Ambitions

(SOMERSET's room of business.)

SOMERSET: Strategically, it's brilliant. Give quarter where it's unimportant, and gather the credit. Keep the reins where it counts.

CLOETE: Governor, it's—

SOMERSET: No no—it's good politics. Fine young mind, Barry, cuts straight to the bone. The abolitionists in London will applaud, their dogs in their laps. They have no notion of what really goes on here. I will bask in the reflection of—

CLOETE: —of young fools run amuck.

SOMERSET: You just wish you'd thought of it. Admit it, Josiah. The winds of change blow up your backside, and you can't bear it.

(BARRY enters. DANTZEN follows, waits in background.)

BARRY: Your Lordship, I've been active since we last met—

SOMERSET: So I understand. But a Bantu woman as orderly? You're turning our prison hospital into an animal kingdom.

BARRY: Not so, Governor, I assure you. Her name is Sibongile. An extraordinary person.

SOMERSET: The Captain had assembled some suitable cand—

BARRY: *(Bows low.)* Mea culpa. Your Lordship.

SOMERSET: *(Looks at CLOETE, laughs.)* Well. I was promised a young, vigourous doctor; I didn't know Lord Buchan was sending a fierce reformer as well.

BARRY: Neither did I, Lord Somerset.

SOMERSET: Explain.

BARRY: I…seem to have *become* one, despite myself.

SOMERSET: Ah.

BARRY: It is the plight of the unfortunates I see all around me. Even prisoners, even lepers! are human beings, deserve our humanity, if nothing else.

SOMERSET: Surely, surely.

BARRY: There are people here, overlooked, daily. The Xhosa, the Malays, the women in the streets—

CLOETE: Barry, you cannot take on every stray dog who crosses your path! Governor, you see how—

SOMERSET: Captain, let me handle this. You are too hot, young man. You must be patient.

BARRY: Forgive me, but… No.

SOMERSET: Thank you, Cloete, that will be all. Barry, send your boy away.

(CLOETE, seething, bows and exits. DANTZEN bows and follows.)

How is he shaping up? You're not encouraging him to get above himself? I counsel strictness, a hard line. To be safe.

BARRY: I am safe with him.

SOMERSET: Don't be too sure. You are small, and slight. You don't mind my observation?

BARRY: With the Warden—I blustered you would back me, as an enlightened leader of the colony's health. I am grateful that you are indeed so.

SOMERSET: I have been so, before you ever arrived on these shores. Despite appearances, I began as you did.

BARRY: I am most presumptuous. Forgive me.

SOMERSET: I do. To my cost, I think. I summon you, you ignore me. I back you up, you take more. You could do murder, young man, and I believe I would turn a blind eye.

BARRY: I try to *save* lives, not take them.

SOMERSET: Then save mine.

(Pause.)

SOMERSET: Shall I tell you how you seem to me? The finest mind I've ever known, in the body of a colt. I advised you, seek protection, and I think you desire it—but you fear it. You mustn't. I have guided the colony, unchallenged, for many years. At last, comes a mind to unsettle me.

BARRY: I thank you for your…indulgence.

SOMERSET: I am just thinking—no, don't go. I will write to the authorities in London for approval in offering you a particular promotion. Nothing to say?

BARRY: I—promotion? I am overwhelmed, Your Lordship.

SOMERSET: You are ambitious; augers well for your future here. I like ambition. I understand it.

BARRY: Thank you, Governor.

SOMERSET: …Are you not curious?

BARRY: It is my most abiding folly.

SOMERSET: James.

BARRY: …Your Lordship?

SOMERSET: Physician to Our Household. Our personal physician.

(They observe each other. CLOETE enters.)

CLOETE: Letter for you. Just arrived.

(BARRY checks the seal. It seems intact. BARRY bows, and exits.)

SOMERSET: What is it?

CLOETE: This heat helps matters, makes the wax pliable. Copy of sales registries, past two years. Kaffir sales.

Scene Eleven Nightmare

(BARRY dreams. A figure, in African mask, dances. MAGGIE, walking.)

BARRY: Maggie? Don't go down there.

(SOMERSET enters dream, in his grinning hunting mask. He caresses BARRY; then intercepts MAGGIE's path, throws MAGGIE backwards, movement of slashing throat, disemboweling her. BARRY wakes, terrified.)

Jesus, Mary and Joseph. Oh Jesus. Dantzen! Dantzen, are you there? Bring a light...

(DANTZEN enters, with a lantern.)

Forgive me. A human face, a voice—not the ones in my head.

DANTZEN: I was awake, meneer.

BARRY: How I dread the nights, dear God. Your people, do they hate us—and who more? Men like me, who are struggling, or the Governor, with his power?

DANTZEN: You are still dreaming.

BARRY: I received this list today, sales registries. Were your family sold?

(DANTZEN doesn't answer.)

They were. Look, what are their names? We will find them.

DANTZEN: Why do you do this. Say these things, make us hope. It was better before.

BARRY: I can change this. If nothing else, I can do that.

DANTZEN: You know nothing of this place, meneer.

BARRY: Then tell me. I am offering to buy them back! God, Dantzen, come on. We can save them.

DANTZEN: *(Angry.)* Her name is Loudrina. We were children together, grew together, worked together—until Galawa was born. My son. Then one day she was sold, before the master died. Out of spite.

BARRY: Surely not.

DANTZEN: You don't understand. He wanted her for his pleasure, and she told him NO—the mother of my boy! When they want us, we pay. Get her out of his sight, sell the woman and child... I hope they are dead, it would be kinder.

BARRY: Oh dear god Dantzen there is such a gaping hole— between things I believe and things that are...

DANTZEN: So you say. But I say, if it's just words, we don't want them.

BARRY: Very well. Deeds. Name—what's her full name, what's she known by? She can't just disappear.

(BARRY scans the lists. MAGGIE appears again.)

DANTZEN: Loudrina Momba. And Galawa, my son. *(Pause.)* It's too late. Too much time has passed. They are dead.

BARRY: No.

DANTZEN: I wear my face. Then I take it off at night, and remember. But my face knows them no more.

BARRY: It's a terrible life, the one you describe.

DANTZEN: The spots on the leopard, the zebra's stripes. To hide in the shadows, or leap above pain. It's protection, doctor. Both of us, in this house. Both Two-Faced.

BARRY: Why—are you looking at me like that.

DANTZEN: I know. You should know that I know. You are a woman.

(BARRY, frozen. MAGGIE disappears.)

BARRY: Don't betray me.

DANTZEN: Who knows your story?

BARRY: No one. No one here.

DANTZEN: The creature I speak of, the Two-Faced? There's no back, only front. But, we said to our boy, never forget—somewhere, inside, a heart beats. I'm protecting my family. You will not use them. For I have found where *you* are soft.

BARRY: It's almost a relief. Ten years I've learned and waited and practised. A hard joy in my gut: they don't know! Sometimes I'm terrified—do they still stone witches to death, I think? So many horrible deaths. I've come too far, I won't ever go back.

DANTZEN: So. We understand each other.

BARRY: Yes.

(She picks up the list again.)

DANTZEN: This idea of yours, for my wife and my son—they could suffer for them. Do you understand *that*?

BARRY: I'm beginning to.

DANTZEN: And I am also saying, be careful. I'm getting used to you. Don't want another master. Don't want another death.

BARRY: *(Nods.)* It's their safety we must ensure. *(She sees:)* Momba. Loudrina. Here, right here! Sold to one Daniel De Groot, August 13, 1820. I will begin by writing De Groot. I will ask him to consider...selling her. And the boy. To me. You agree?

(After a moment, DANTZEN nods.)

You are dangerous to me.

DANTZEN: It is mutual.

BARRY: You could give me away.

DANTZEN: Who would believe me. Doctor sir.

Scene Twelve Love Life

(Night. SOMERSET and CLOETE with brandy.)

CLOETE: —a letter from Daniel de Groot. On his way to Madagascar, an opportunity there. Taking his household with him. He asks why our little doctor sticks his nose in his business. Out of the blue Barry writes to him wanting his kaffir boy. Bloody nerve!

SOMERSET: Have you asked Barry why?

CLOETE: No indeed. *(Sudden shock.)* Your Lordship, you don't suppose he's—!

SOMERSET: You've a filthy mind, Josiah. I'm glad you're not English, I'd be forced to dismiss you. You've done well, eh—for an Afrikaaner. Fine horses, fine wines.

CLOETE: I have...hopes, as you know... Miss Georgiana—

SOMERSET: Oh you can do better, my daughter's a featherhead.

CLOETE: You are cruel, Your Lordship.

SOMERSET: It's the heat. I listen to the lions, and long to roar myself.

CLOETE: *(Confused.)* Ja. We need rain.

SOMERSET: Love, man, love! *(He paces, restless.)* Perhaps not you. Bloodless as my daughter. Perhaps you *would* suit her.

CLOETE: I am sure I would.

SOMERSET: She lies in of an afternoon, claims she has headaches. Calls for Dr. Barry; it's absurd how she dotes on him. Eh, Josiah—women. I am bored here, I tell you. Deadly.

CLOETE: The colony has a million eyes, Governor.

SOMERSET: But only one way of seeing the world.

CLOETE: One official way.

SOMERSET: Mm, through the small end. Like a fart through a corset. Barry's like a son, hm? A son of sorts.

CLOETE: I tell you, people are not blind. You've never given so freely, been so generous—and your tailor, the expenses!—

SOMERSET: You are jealous, Cloete! I'm touched.

CLOETE: I am not! It is just—he goes over my head, Governor, comes straight to you. Blowing things out of proportion, writing letters like a madman—

SOMERSET: Now as for this letter, he's very prolific,—what, after all, is a kaffir or two between gentlemen? If Barry wants this particular boy, why doesn't De Groot let him have him. The Dutch must stop being greedy, give up one or two luxuries, in the interests of equity. *(With a sly smile.)* Oh, I beg your pardon. You are Dutch as well. I keep forgetting. You are so much one of us.

Scene Thirteen Sister

(Leper colony. BARRY and DANTZEN with PROSTITUTE, who is in constant pain.)

BARRY: I've counselled the Brothers you should work in the garden—not too strenuous, but fresh air is good for you.

PROSTITUTE: Make her work on her feet now she's no good on her back. What you send me way up here for, die with the cripples. What's yer boy's name?

DANTZEN: It is Dantzen.

PROSTITUTE: Speaks for himself. So that's why you weren't interested. You'd rather bugger.

BARRY: You're a filthy creature, now stop it!

PROSTITUTE: Makes you sorry for feelin' sorry, does it?

BARRY: Do you read, have you read?

PROSTITUTE: Sure I read, what d'you think? Once upon a time and all.

BARRY: Then you know Shakespeare.

PROSTITUTE: That jemmy fellow.

BARRY: I'll bring you him.

PROSTITUTE: I'd rather have *you*, dear. Bit warmer.

(BARRY turns to go.)

So what was she called then, this sister o' yours?

BARRY: She was called Maggie.

PROSTITUTE: And what'd she die of? In a soft bed, in childbirth?

BARRY: She died when I was busy.

PROSTITUTE: Fine brother you are.

DANTZEN: Coming, doctor?

PROSTITUTE: In a minute, don't rush him. Tell me, darlin', eh?

BARRY: I'd been in Edinburgh, become a doctor. We hadn't much money. What I had I sent home, I... Returned to London, she was missing. My mother didn't know where. Didn't much care. The money was to have been for them both. I was interning, Sir Astley Cooper. He's a researcher, needs cadavers. Sent along to the morgue, I—

(BARRY stops, arrested in memory.)

PROSTITUTE: She'd been on the streets then? Her throat was slashed?

BARRY: And other—other... She had struggled. Then crawled. She was eighteen. Seven months pregnant.

PROSTITUTE: Jesus. I could feel that. To be, then not, that's the bloody question. See, I know me Shakespeare.

(Kisses BARRY.)

And I still know I'm dyin'.

(She exits.)

DANTZEN: So this is your dream.

BARRY: There must be something—some plant, some root, if we could find it, use it fearlessly, against disease, even death. Especially death. What are you thinking about?

DANTZEN: My thoughts are still my own.

BARRY: I'm tired. I'm glad you're here. I'm glad you know.

DANTZEN: Yes.

Scene Fourteen Heat

        (SOMERSET's room of business. BARRY enters, dusty from riding, followed by DANTZEN. SOMERSET dismisses CLOETE, eyes on BARRY.)

CLOETE: *(Sotto voce.)* Like a magnet. All points lead to you.

        (CLOETE clicks his heels, exits. SOMERSET also dismisses DANTZEN.)

SOMERSET: You've been gone two weeks.

        (He approaches BARRY.)

        How have you done it? How have you come so far? So fast?

BARRY: I…I'm a hard worker. And hard work is rewarded—

SOMERSET: You're a liar, doctor; consummate skill. No more games now. What makes your heart race? What keeps you awake nights? Hm? I'm not a sleeper, prowl the grounds. Have you ventured? Out at night? I could show you such things as you've never dreamed Horatio—you like Shakespeare, don't you? Like all "new gentlemen". Oh yes, I know many things, James, that you wish to keep hidden. Ah, I have your full attention now. Answer. Why are you drawn to me?

BARRY: I am not yet—skilful—in this…

SOMERSET: 'Course you are, every day. I have missed you while you were away—

        (SOMERSET strokes BARRY's cheek.)

        —your white skin. How long do you think this can continue?

BARRY: I don't know what you mean.

SOMERSET: Oh yes you do. I could have ended it long before now, but the game's advancing. Keep up with me. *(Calls.)* Cloete! *(To BARRY.)* Struwig's been moved up, Inspector General. He'll be terrible; we'll retire him soon.

(CLOETE enters.)

(To CLOETE.) Another promotion! *(To BARRY.)* London's kept us waiting for confirmation of your first—we'll dispense with formalities in this case and simply go ahead. In good faith.

CLOETE: I'm not quite...with you, Your Excellency.

SOMERSET: Chief Medical Inspector for Cape Town and District. Dr. Barry. See to the paperwork. Raise in pay, raise in status. You'll have to work harder, Captain, to keep up with our meteor. Eh?

BARRY: *(Shocked.)* Lord Somerset—

SOMERSET: Good day, gentlemen.

(CLOETE clicks his heels.)

We must cure you of that, Cloete. It's not quite us.

(SOMERSET exits.)

CLOETE: Yirra, Barry. You seem agitated.

BARRY: No more than usual.

CLOETE: Overworking you, are we?

BARRY: Not at all. But the Governor shouldn't—

CLOETE: Lord Somerset accepts the guidance of no one, you should know that.

BARRY: Not even you?

CLOETE: Especially not me. The wind changes quickly here. Never lasts long. Up and down like a doxy's damned skirts.

BARRY: Then stop him.

CLOETE: Am I my Governor's keeper? I think not. If I was, I'd be clearer in my directives to you, for one.

BARRY: Oh yes? And what would you say, were you his keeper?

CLOETE: I would start with a recommendation to you to return to England, where your fascination, such as it is, could be appreciated—

BARRY: Still prickling about Lady Georgiana?

CLOETE: —And then I would tell you you were a meddling, unscrupulous little shit!

(He pulls BARRY's nose.)

BARRY: Apologize for that!

CLOETE: I shall not.

BARRY: Apologize!

CLOETE: Careful cocky—I'm the best marksman in the Cape, /and I only say what everyone knows to be truth.

BARRY: I'll have your liver and your lights, on a platter and for breakfast!

(CLOETE snorts derisively, turns to leave.)

Sunup! The oaks at Alphen. Sabres, or pistols, your choice.

CLOETE: Neither. I'd win.

BARRY: You decline to fight me, you big ugly dandy?

CLOETE: Pistols!

Barry, Cloete and Somerset

Cloete, Seconds and Barry

Photo by Norma Rodgers

Scene Fifteen The Duel

        (Fog. A clearing.)

BARRY: Where is the man.

DANTZEN: Perhaps he thought better of it.

BARRY: He's gun-mad. Can't wait to take a shot at me.

DANTZEN: You court death like a lover. It seems to me—

BARRY: I don't have the least interest /in what it seems to you—

DANTZEN: —that you do it as you do everything. On sinew alone. That the sinew will finally crack. That it can't take the strain.

BARRY: Be quiet.

        (Pause.)

DANTZEN: What shall I do with your body. It is a problem. I could leave it to them. Then they shall know what your secret is. I could take it away, let the lions destroy it. And be killed for my carelessness.

BARRY: Dantzen—

DANTZEN: —Or I could warn you. As I do. When you court death alone, know who you may be facing. His embrace is long and tight. *(Beat.)* If you die today, I shall run.

        (CLOETE enters, with a SECOND. They nod, prepare, stand back to back, and pace off, pistols upraised.)

SECOND: Gentlemen. You shall take eight paces, turn, and fire. *(Counting.)* One, two, three, four, five, six, seven, eight.

(They turn, fire. Both are shaken, hide it. The SECOND takes the pistol from CLOETE.)

A close shot, sir.

CLOETE: No. No. Nowhere near.

(SECOND takes pistol from BARRY.)

BARRY: Dantzen, fall in now.

CLOETE: Thank you, Kramer. I'll catch you up.

(The SECOND goes on. CLOETE holds out his hand)

All forgiven?

BARRY: It's you who need to forgive me.

CLOETE: Honour satisfied, then.

BARRY: Cold wind this morning. Hardly see to fire.

CLOETE: Mm. You'd like to have killed me, wouldn't you.

BARRY: Don't know what's come over me. Such a fierce rage.

CLOETE: Blood sports. You've got the craving. We're none of us safe now, eh?

(CLOETE slaps BARRY on the back)

Good man! Your ear a moment, on a personal note. So we understand each other. Be off, boy.

(CLOETE gestures, and DANTZEN moves away.)

You attend His Lordship's daughter, Miss Georgiana, do you not?

BARRY: You know I do.

CLOETE: What do you think of her? She seems often to be ailing.

BARRY: Nothing is wrong that a month without men would not cure.

CLOETE: I am determined to have her for my wife.

BARRY: What makes you think she'll have you?

CLOETE: My...position. And I flatter myself that I am not bad looking.

BARRY: Your Van Dyck, particularly. Stupendous.

CLOETE: You couldn't grow one to save your life! And I'll sire more sons than you'll ever deliver. So be warned. She is mine.

BARRY: Captain. You are right, on all counts. But the wind of my charge still rustled through your scalp, and every bristle stood on end, you can't deny it.

CLOETE: *(Stiff.)* I'm not the talker you are. The way she dances with you, and laughs—your medical visits—

BARRY: She admires my waistcoats.

CLOETE: —and your inexpressibles. Why do you wear them so tight, Barry, you're practically obscene.

BARRY: You'd wear them yourself if you dared.

(Pause.)

CLOETE: He's right; you *do* keep us on our toes.

BARRY: *(Wary.)* Spoken about me, have you?

CLOETE: *(Also wary.)* Now and again.

BARRY: And what do you think of him. In all honesty.

CLOETE: What do I think? He's a man-eater.

BARRY: Yes.

CLOETE: And I have survived him. You will too. Kindly remember what I have told you.

(CLOETE turns to go.)

BARRY: —I was lucky. Or you were faking.

CLOETE: Not true. We almost died there. Over a woman.

BARRY: Not over a woman.

	(Pause.)
CLOETE:	Another thing then. Since we understand each other. Be careful of expenditures, especially now. London's sending a man to investigate him. Keep your nose clean. For his is very dirty, ja? Good morning, Barry. Good fighting.
	(He exits. DANTZEN returns. BARRY begins to shake.)
DANTZEN:	You're hurt?
BARRY:	No. Let me sit down, before I—
DANTZEN:	Why did you challenge him?
BARRY:	The Governor *knows*, I am sure of it.
DANTZEN:	And if he does?
BARRY:	This will show him he's wrong.
DANTZEN:	You are cracking now, sinew showing, I can see it.
BARRY:	Every day, every second. Do they spend all their lives, always proving?
DANTZEN:	Not all of them. But you do.
BARRY:	Dear God...
DANTZEN:	You can't be rock and then water, if they're not to know.
BARRY:	You're going to leave me!
DANTZEN:	Meneer. Cape Town is like a lion's jaws. Not many places for a man to hide. I may *want* to run, but I can wait for death.
	(BARRY hugs DANTZEN. He holds her firmly away.)
	No.
	(BARRY exits.)
	Galawa... I feel new hungers. I don't know what to do with them. Don't test me too far.

Scene Sixteen   The Bedchamber

(SOMERSET's bedroom. Tiger hide on the floor. SOMERSET, in a nightshirt, in bed. Early evening.)

CLOETE: Better shot than I gave him credit for.

SOMERSET: Thought he might be. And he?

CLOETE: Sure I grazed him. But then, not sure. He didn't show it, if so.

SOMERSET: I've summoned him. Open the window, or I'll be scolded for lack of ventilation.

CLOETE: *(Going to window.)* Yirra. We can't clear our throats in the mess without Barry barking orders at us not to spit. Yet he's right about that too—fewer flies.

SOMERSET: We'll be working into the evening.

CLOETE: In this heat!

SOMERSET: I'm resting, never fear. Besides, Barry loves it. He told me so.

CLOETE: Little bugger.

(BARRY enters, resplendent.)

SOMERSET: Speak of the devil, in full dress kit.

BARRY: Captain. If you please.

(BARRY crosses to window, throws it open. SOMERSET is amused. CLOETE looks at both, speculatively, then goes out.)

Now then. How are you feeling?

66   Tiger's Heart

SOMERSET: Better. Steadily better.

BARRY: Coddling yourself too much?

SOMERSET: In what way, doctor?

BARRY: Eating to excess? Meat? Fowl? What vegetables did you have today?

SOMERSET: Why, none.

BARRY: *That* will be the death of you, Governor. Fat gourmets need exercise—you should try living on a shilling a day and *earning* it, that's the way to remain healthy.

SOMERSET: Enough. Official sanction from England's arrived: "Physician to Our Household." A great honour, at this stage in your career.

BARRY: I am grateful, Your Lordship.

SOMERSET: You are already accepted as such. However, this also entitles you to residence in Government House cottage. Just across the grounds.

BARRY: And?

SOMERSET: And an additional 1200 rix dollars a year. As you are already aware.

BARRY: I like to hear it, Governor. Forgive me.

SOMERSET: You irritate me as much as you fascinate me, Barry.

BARRY: Thank you. I shall move in immediately.

SOMERSET: Your quarrel with Cloete ended satisfactorily?

BARRY: We cleared the air, yes.

SOMERSET: Glad you're still with us.

BARRY: A surprise to you?

SOMERSET: I reserved judgement.

   (Pause.)

You know why I sent for you.

BARRY: I am your physician.

SOMERSET: You *know* why I sent for you. Today.

BARRY: I'm not sure...

SOMERSET: You know.

(Pause.)

BARRY: Yes.

SOMERSET: Come here.

BARRY: I am...

SOMERSET: I will be gentle.

BARRY: ...I fear this. And yet...

SOMERSET: It's been a good chase.

(BARRY moves to the bed. SOMERSET reaches for BARRY, kisses her, moves to unbutton her jacket.)

Help me. *(Outside, a pair of monkeys begin to screech.)* It's only the jackos.

BARRY: *(Moves to window, calls.)* Dantzen? Go home, will you? I shall be some time.

(SOMERSET follows BARRY, kisses her, caresses her cheek.)

SOMERSET: So smooth—

(He reaches for BARRY's shirt front.)

BARRY: Wait.

SOMERSET: Just those, then.

(BARRY undoes her trousers.)

BARRY: Yes. I knew this was coming. I have told myself, no. Put my secret in your hands, it is madness, and yet—I have dreamt of you.

SOMERSET: And I of you.

BARRY: Please...

(SOMERSET, kissing BARRY, runs his hands over BARRY's body, down the thighs, between the legs. He realizes.)

What is it?

SOMERSET: What—

BARRY: Is something wrong?

SOMERSET: By god, Barry—

(Pause.)

BARRY: ...I thought you knew.

SOMERSET: By god!

(Pause.)

I hope...I'm the only one.

BARRY: Who *knows*? Of course you are. ...Am *I*?

SOMERSET: Are you what.

BARRY: The only one here who knows. Of *you*?

SOMERSET: *I* am not the one with unusual appetites—I would say yours are insatiably perverse! Good God, what were you thinking of?

BARRY: The same as you. The very same! I thought you knew!

SOMERSET: No, by god, if I had I'd—! Where did you come from.

BARRY: Why does this interest you? I've *done* it.

SOMERSET: This is inconceivable! Does Lord Buchan know?

BARRY: He helped me, encouraged me.

SOMERSET: I shall write to him, I shall—

BARRY: What shall you say? I have done my job, and done it well. It is only now, when confronted with my body, when it is not what you wanted... Don't be a coward, I beg you.

SOMERSET: Let me see that face. How have you done it. The facts, Barry, the facts.

BARRY: Very well. Born of a poor woman, who married badly, twice. Ran away with us to my uncle, a painter, Royal Academy. He had patrons, before he died. I came up with a plan—outrageous, but possible. I was a plain girl.

SOMERSET: And a plainer woman.

BARRY: This is *my* story, not yours to amend. I had a good brain and Lord Buchan backed me—I was the adventure he'd never had. Only one way to enter medicine—and I did it, I've done it. On my own merit. I am a gentleman.

(SOMERSET turns away.)

You no longer want me. I see. You're a widower, two daughters, I assumed— As you say, I'm very green. …No, I see what it is. After all these months, all this—hunger—I'm to stay as I am. While you can devour whatever you please.

SOMERSET: Very well, Barry, we are starving together. Do you want me?

BARRY: Yes.

SOMERSET: You will have me.

BARRY: Yes!

(He caresses her, pulling down her trousers, then thrusts into her from behind.)

BARRY: Ah! I will bleed.

SOMERSET: Don't talk… Ohhh… You little…witch…

(BARRY gasps; it is fast, and hard, but this is not a rape. He moves away.)

BARRY: What did you call me?

SOMERSET: That is nothing. Nothing.

BARRY: It didn't hurt.

SOMERSET: You didn't bleed.

(BARRY pulls up her trousers.)

BARRY: I'd heard there was more. I feel their hunger, the women—dance with me, doctor me, heal me. Is this what they want?

SOMERSET: Enough! Your big mouth, that should have been the clue.

BARRY: When did you change, Governor?

SOMERSET: Ask: when did I return. My wife's death. Sometimes I like it soft. Sometimes hard. I thought I'd found another human being to make life bearable, for a little while. You could have fought me. So much more interesting. Shall we try again? You are shocked. You wanted love. I thought you were above that.

BARRY: I am speechless.

SOMERSET: For once. *(Pause.)* I could expose you.

BARRY: The best mind in your colony. Keep my secret. And I will keep yours. It *is* a hanging offense.

SOMERSET: By God, little rat. You should be pulling up trousers and getting the hell out, hoping for mercy from high places. This colony is mine. No one will listen to your little voice.

BARRY: Maybe not here, they wouldn't dare. But back in England.

SOMERSET: You don't want to go back to England. Don't you ever play the game with me—you're out of your depth. Stick to bodies and blood, what you're trained for. *(Stroking her.)* So you thought I knew. You must have been hungry to risk it. Come on then. Again. The flesh may be different, but the heart of this animal, it's what I expected, I could swear to it.

(He kisses her. She does not pull away. CLOETE knocks.)

CLOETE: Governor?

SOMERSET: Yes, by god.

(BARRY crosses to the door. CLOETE is outside.)

CLOETE: Before you go. A letter.

(He passes over a letter, and points to an unbuttoned button.)

Promotion can be painful, ja?

(BARRY hastens away. The TRACKER appears, above, with a letter.)

TRACKER: "To Dr. James Barry. From Daniel De Groot. Madagascar. The kaffir, Loudrina. Dead in childbirth." It was De Groot's. "The boy Galawa...sold to a trader...bound for Nepal." Yes I was. *(In Xhosa:) Ngaphambi ko'ba sibe lapha, sasi phaya. Ngaphambi ko'ba sibe phaya, sasi kwenye indawo. Ngaphambi koko sasi ngenamhlaba.* [Before we were here, we were there. Before we were there, we were elsewhere. Before we were elsewhere, we were nowhere.] I've found you now, mlungu. White woman now man. You're still like them.

(End of ACT ONE.)

Somerset and Barry

Photo by Norma Rodgers

ACT II

Scene Seventeen Watchdog

(Two months later. The TRACKER watches, in light and shadow, moving back into the world. Hemel and Aarde, the leper colony.)

BARRY: Your attention. I am Dr. James Barry, Chief Medical Inspector for Cape Town and District. As physician to one of your number, a young woman with many...sorrows...I tried to heal her body, but she died alone, despairing, without a place for her soul.

To all of you at the Hemel and Aarde, I hereby vow to make your lives bearable. Better food, better hygiene, better care for your needs. You are suffering from a terrible ailment for which we do not yet know a cure. I do not see why you should be hungry or maltreated—you are being punished enough for sins unknown. I will be your watchdog. This I swear.

(BARRY exits. The TRACKER, about to follow, moves again into background as SOMERSET appears.)

Scene Eighteen   Heal Thyself

(Dappled light of a shade tree, grounds of Government House. SOMERSET has a riding whip.)

SOMERSET: You've been avoiding me. It's a merry game—you're a master deceiver. No one need know—you must come to me again.

BARRY: Your Lordship. I am—with child.

SOMERSET: For Christ's sake!

(He paces, swishing his whip.)

BARRY: I—I was sure it was overwork, that any day—

SOMERSET: I cannot believe that a single coupling—

BARRY: Your anatomy, and timing, are in perfect working order, Governor.

SOMERSET: By god, you're a self-righteous little prick.

BARRY: You know I am not that.

SOMERSET: You're a doctor. Do something.

BARRY: I don't know what you expect me to do. Any midwife would spread the news far and wide. And I can't do it alone.

SOMERSET: Why not?

BARRY: I'd die.

(SOMERSET paces, swishing the whip. BARRY watches him.)

You feel nothing? What if I want it?—what if I do?

SOMERSET: I don't believe that for a moment.

BARRY: It's a problem, yes, I'll admit that I'm frightened—

SOMERSET: It will make me a laughing stock, and you a foolish, ugly spinster. I will never allow myself to be laughed at, do you hear me? And *you* will never recover.

BARRY: I could learn to.

SOMERSET: To grow large and heavy? To feel soft stirrings? Oh no, little rat. Even hidden away, some mysterious ailment, news would leak. James Barry gives birth? It's intolerable.

BARRY: It seems so, indeed.

SOMERSET: If you let this out, your life as a doctor, as *any*thing of consequence, is over—and you won't do that, you're too ambitious. Go back to your Hemel and Aarde, carry on there. You say you want to find a cure—so find one! Come back with a child—however explained—say goodbye to your career, and your name. You can go up, or very quickly down.

BARRY: You are famous, you know. Among your men as much as your women.

SOMERSET: *(he grabs her around the throat)* I'll kill you, Barry, do you hear me? I'll kill you with my bare hands if you allow this to become known.

BARRY: I believe you would, Governor.

(SOMERSET turns to go.)

Physician, heal thyself.

SOMERSET: What?

BARRY: May I wish you luck, at the hunt?

SOMERSET: You may.

(He strides off, calling.)

Bring that horse! Now! Look lively, boy!

Scene Nineteen Bodies and Blood

(BARRY's cottage, night. DANTZEN enters.)

DANTZEN: Weren't you sleeping, meneer?

BARRY: No. And yes, I've been drinking, mind your business. I don't feel well.

DANTZEN: You shouldn't drink, meneer. You need your strength, eh?

BARRY: Oh God. I don't want it.

DANTZEN: But it's coming just the same.

BARRY: I hate it.

DANTZEN: You don't mean that. We can do it. Go somewhere other, the Hemel and Aarde. Say it is research. I will help you.

(BARRY puts her head down and weeps.)

BARRY: It's all over.

DANTZEN: You should tell me things. Back and forth, I tell you, you tell me.

BARRY: I've been such a fool. I thought he knew.

DANTZEN: *(He realizes.)* The Governor.

(BARRY nods)

DANTZEN: *(Xhosa:) Ngaphambi ko'ba sibe phaya, sasi kwenye indawo.* [Before we were there, we were elsewhere.] Go to bed, meneer. In the morning. We will think then.

BARRY: You blame me for Loudrina. And Galawa.

DANTZEN:	Come on now.
BARRY:	Everything I touch has gone wrong.
DANTZEN:	Stop this. You are what I have left now. So stop this.
	(Pause.)
BARRY:	Very well. I will. Goodnight, Dantzen.

(He exits. MAGGIE enters, walking, blood at her throat. BARRY watches her.)

Was he handsome, and strong? Did it begin well, Maggie? Did he love you—or shove you up against the side of a building? How did it happen?

(MAGGIE lifting her white gown, above her knees.)

Cold in the morgue, sweetheart. Colder than hell.

(MAGGIE hears a male whistle, poses seductively.)

It wasn't safe. You thought you'd be safe.

(MAGGIE exits, following her fate. BARRY drinks.)

I won't go back. Jesus. I'm frightened. Be with me now, and at the hour of my death.

(BARRY removes boots and pants, picks up a long narrow surgical instrument. She sits on edge of desk, feet on a chair; aborts herself. DANTZEN hears her scream; enters to find her covered in blood, in shock.)

DANTZEN:	Let go of that! I will go for Sibongile, she'll help us here. Why'd you do this? Why'd you keep it to yourself?
	(She grabs his hand.)
BARRY:	Am I a monster, Dantzen?
DANTZEN:	I'm not a Christian, to see your monsters. Hold on, meneer.

(He exits, running.)

Scene Twenty Troublemaker

(CLOETE, reading a letter SOMERSET has dictated.)

CLOETE: "2nd April, 1822. Dearest Mary: I cannot tell you how delighted I shall be to host your visit to our colony. Of course, you must reside at Government House. You shall thrill to the lions and smile at the jackos, as I did, and do, every day. This land is full of surprises, and savagery, but I shall make every effort to subdue those elements in honour of your beauty and your graciousness. As always, yours, Charles Somerset." Stunning, Your Lordship.

SOMERSET: I hope so.

(BARRY at the leper colony, still pale, writing a letter.)

BARRY: "From the Hemel and Aarde, Cape Town District. To: Army Medical Department, London, 17th August, 1822. Honoured Sirs: It has come to my attention that His Excellency the Governor has written to request I be posted elsewhere for reasons of health. I am writing to *demand* my continuance at the Cape, and to assure you that I am in perfect physical and mental condition. I will *not* be curtailed nor cut off from my patients, from the life I have attained, in this my adopted—and preferred!—home. If Lord Somerset feels strongly, let *him* depart! Let *him* begin again! Let *him* feel the consequences!"

(She drinks. The internal injury informs her movement for the rest of the play.)

TRACKER: "There was once a friendship between a big cat and a forest, who lived together in harmony. After a while the cat caused problems. He and the forest grew violently opposed. He left with a lash of his muscular tail, and the forest pulled its leaves close and felt glad. One day, the villagers discovered the cat was no longer friends with the forest. So they came with their axes and they chopped the forest down. Then they went to the plain, where the animal was panting in the sun. He tried to hide, but there was no leafy shelter to disappear into. He also was killed." Then what did you tell me, father? "The cat and the forest were safer when they were friends—but they did not know it." Could you not feel it coming?

Scene Twenty One The Return

(Outside the steps of Government House. CLOETE takes snuff. BARRY hurries by, with a cane.)

CLOETE: Barry, welcome back.

BARRY: Thank you.

CLOETE: Find a cure?

BARRY: There is no cure for leprosy. I was naive to think it. Time to take up the gauntlet again in this vale of sin.

CLOETE: Reminds me—have you heard? A distant cousin from England. May keep him occupied for a bit yet.

BARRY: What.

CLOETE: Married. Three months ago—you didn't know? A quiet ceremony, at the estate, only two hundred guests. No expenses spared. He's diverted your budget, by almost half—and he'll need to raise taxes again, that'll cause mayhem. Don't look so shocked. Where do you think he got his thoroughbreds? Financed Government House and all the grounds? Never mind, the watchers are here.

BARRY: Who—?

CLOETE: That would be telling. He's clever, however. Seen it before, when his first wife died. Like Cromwell he turns, suddenly pious. My guess is he's after a son. By the way, what kept you? Thought you'd contracted it yourself, you were so long among them.

BARRY: Dysentery.

CLOETE: Nasty. Lost all your colour. And the cane?

BARRY: It is nothing.

CLOETE: Soon be back in fighting trim, ja?

BARRY: Very soon, I trust.

CLOETE: No lost noses, bits of you missing? Wouldn't want to be without a duellist, life could get too bloody dull, hey? Look sharp. Here he is.

(SOMERSET enters, LADY MARY on his arm. She carries a parasol.)

SOMERSET: Gentlemen. My love, this is our famous doctor, James Barry. My lady wife.

BARRY: Lady Somerset. Welcome to Cape Town.

LADY MARY: I thank you.

CLOETE: Your Ladyship.

SOMERSET: If you'll excuse us, gentlemen. My wife is in a delicate state and must not become overtired.

(SOMERSET and LADY SOMERSET exit.)

BARRY: She's pregnant.

CLOETE: How can you tell? You should settle, settle into life here. Marry, have children—

BARRY: I have fewer options, Cloete, believe me; I have only a few.

CLOETE: Such as.

BARRY: Power, if you're interested.

CLOETE: Women are safer.

BARRY: Not for me.

CLOETE: Suit yourself. But you'll be a lonely man.

(They look after SOMERSET.)

Smiling like a shark, and soon to be a pappy.

BARRY: Christ.

CLOETE: Oh to be rich. And British.

Scene Twenty Two Power

> *(The next day. SOMERSET, and BARRY. Both are nervous.)*

SOMERSET: So? All is well?

BARRY: As you see.

SOMERSET: Good. Good. You look terrible. I suppose you know that.

BARRY: Why are you trying to send me away?

SOMERSET: For your own good. And mine.

BARRY: This is my home now, as it is yours. It's a big country. We are civilized beings.

SOMERSET: You would do better elsewhere.

BARRY: I do very well here.

SOMERSET: I don't want to see you.

BARRY: Then let me travel the district, get away from the centre. From you.

SOMERSET: You are Chief Medical Inspector. You'll go no higher, not in my colony, I can promise you. That's what you've come back for, isn't it? Well, isn't it?

BARRY: Leave me alone, and I will leave you alone. Just give me a free rein, for God's sake.

SOMERSET: You amuse me, Barry. The day I give you free rein is the day I am dead, socially and politically.

BARRY: Consider: it will reflect well to have your Chief Medical Inspector fighting *for* you, not against you.

SOMERSET: You will soon be transferred.

BARRY: No I will not.

SOMERSET: Was it terrible? *Was* it? I thought of you, nightly, that flat little belly, imagined you thickening, how you'd hate it. Can't imagine you crying. Do you cry, little rat? Did you cry out? You're a Catholic—did you suffer?

BARRY: It is dead. That is all.

SOMERSET: Come to me again. Come and I'll stroke you. Feel you arch your back against me.

BARRY: You have a wife!

SOMERSET: But you were mine first. You could be everything, James—we could have it all.

BARRY: I will fight you, I will hurt you—I will do such things, what they are I know not but they shall be the terrors of the earth!

SOMERSET: You told me once you were a gentleman. Behave like one.

BARRY: I'm to know when to fawn and scrape, and when to crawl away nicely? Like Captain Cloete?

SOMERSET: You've lost your mind, Barry, as well as your shape.

BARRY: I am a man, expect me to make demands like a man—

SOMERSET: /You are no man!

BARRY: —a man who can match you step for bloody step! I want it, I've worked for it—make me Inspector General, you bastard!

SOMERSET: Never!

(CLOETE enters)

CLOETE: Barry, thank heaven I caught you. It's Lady Somerset, she's feeling unwell. Her Lady's maid has asked that Barry be sent for, Your Lordship.

SOMERSET: Call for Dr. Struwig.

CLOETE: She's asked for Barry. He *is* Physician of Your Household.

(They enter MARY's chamber; CLOETE goes.)

SOMERSET: Mary. The doctor is here.

BARRY: Where does it hurt, Lady Somerset?

SOMERSET: Everywhere. The light hurts her eyes, she can't seem to move.

BARRY: I asked her Ladyship. *(To MARY.)* Lean forward, please. When was the last time you took exercise?

SOMERSET: Answer the doctor.

LADY MARY: I...walk in the gardens. I paint, a little. But I should not be too active, should I doctor?

BARRY: Moderately. It's good for you.

SOMERSET: Her physician in England—

BARRY: I am her physician now. *(To MARY.)* You eat fruit?

LADY MARY: Lord Somerset does not like it.

BARRY: So *you* do not eat it?

LADY MARY: ...No.

BARRY: Governor, you'll excuse us?

SOMERSET: She is my wife.

BARRY: A physician and his patient is like a priest and his parishioner. There must be privacy, even from God.

(SOMERSET goes, with ill grace.)

Now. You must eat, and do, what is good for *you*. This is a harsh land. You must obey its necessities, and leave those of the old one behind, if you are to survive. If your baby is to survive. This is your first child, yes?

LADY MARY: Yes. I am frightened. I married late, as you see. I was the baby of the family. I have not been around children, I

	don't know what they need and…well. I must be boring you.
BARRY:	I assure you, you are not.
LADY MARY:	Dr. Barry, you are young, you came here alone, is that so?
BARRY:	Very much so.
LADY MARY:	How do you manage.
BARRY:	Rather badly, I'm afraid. *(Rising.)* I will come tomorrow, bring some of the excellent fruit available. It will ease your discomfort. And you must walk, take the air.
LADY MARY:	What time tomorrow will you come?
BARRY:	Early.
LADY MARY:	I am awake at five.
BARRY:	I am not. *(Bows.)* Lady Somerset.

(BARRY leaves the bedroom. SOMERSET approaches.)

She is lovely.

SOMERSET:	This is exactly what I do not want. Struwig was perfectly satisfactory before you came. I allowed her to see you against my better judgement; it will not happen again. You are no longer Physician to Our Household, do you understand me?
BARRY:	Completely. I will hope we can manage; with people between us we remember our manners. I will keep a crowd at my heels at all times.
SOMERSET:	I don't need your insubordination.
BARRY:	Just my skill. You may need that.

(SOMERSET exits. DANTZEN joins BARRY. They look at each other, and he puts a hand on her shoulder.)

Barry and the Prostitute

Somerset, Lady Mary and Barry

Scene Twenty Three What's the Cost?

>*(Six months later. SOMERSET and CLOETE, with brandy. US, SOMERSET's bedchamber; BARRY attends MARY in labour. A scream.)*

SOMERSET: Jesus Christ, Josiah! Is there no end to it? The woman will die before she births, at this rate.

CLOETE: Your Excellency, please.

SOMERSET: How has he done it? London refuses to transfer him—bows to his wishes. Struwig calls for him, against my express orders—

CLOETE: Younger man, smaller hands. In an emergency—

SOMERSET: He will kill her!

CLOETE: He's her only hope. In fact. The Home Office is...wondering. First you promote him, then you... Well. His clinic's overflowing, he's very popular and—I assure you, Her Ladyship has the best of men. *(He watches SOMERSET pacing.)* I...don't know what you want me to tell you. Your Lordship.

SOMERSET: For Christ's sake, it's simple. Are you with me, or with him.

>*(MARY cries out. SOMERSET drinks.)*

CLOETE: *(Nervous.)* I am your Aide-de-Camp, Governor. I never forget my title, my allegiance.

SOMERSET: He's driving me mad! Keep an eye on him for me; what he says, who he sees. Especially who he sees. Do you follow?

CLOETE: Your Lordship.

SOMERSET: Thank God for your steadiness. *(He drinks.)* We'll be giving a ball after my lady's recovery. Georgiana's still pining. Perhaps—if it is not too galling...

CLOETE: I'm an excellent fellow.

SOMERSET: Perhaps I've misjudged you.

CLOETE: Perhaps.

(He eyes SOMERSET, who looks haunted. BARRY enters.)

BARRY: She's lost strength, there's no more. I have to perform surgery.

SOMERSET: Surgery? Are you insane?

BARRY: The baby's presentation's all wrong, I can't turn it. Straining for hours, she's exhausted. I will be making an incision into the abdomen and the baby will enter the world a new way, yes? Cloete, take him out.

SOMERSET: You expect me to go quietly—

(MARY cries out.)

—while you carve her up! Now do you see—

BARRY: She will die, and the baby will die, if it is not delivered immediately.

CLOETE: Come with me. Barry knows what he's doing. Come, Sir Charles, you'll never forgive yourself—

(MARY screams again. BARRY returns to bedchamber.)

SOMERSET: Oh God. Women die, Cloete, they die of this, often. I will be blamed. Bringing her here.

CLOETE: Trust him. Stay calm now.

SOMERSET: An innocent pawn. What has she to do with this savagery. What does she know of this—place?

(The TRACKER, in a separate place, remembering his father, and himself as a small boy:)

TRACKER: This is where you told me, right here by this tree—"you'll grow to be strong, Galawa. Don't be afraid. Come here to me. Closer. You are almost there."

(The TRACKER disappears. SOMERSET in the bedchamber, with MARY and the newborn. He helps her drink brandy. BARRY in the antechamber, with CLOETE.)

LADY MARY: ...Alive... Oh my darling. Alive.

BARRY: A boy.

LADY MARY: My little son.

(SOMERSET kisses MARY.)

BARRY: A son, very healthy. But we're not out of the woods. Risk of infection. And terrible pain from the incision.

CLOETE: An incision you say? I've never heard of that, Barry. In cold blood, and on purpose?

BARRY: Only way to save her.

SOMERSET: *(Moving through antechamber, to BARRY.)* I could have you court-martialled. Do what you need to do for her and go.

(He exits.)

CLOETE: Done this before have you?

BARRY: Never. Saw it once, in Scotland. During my training. Caesarian section. Right through the abdominal wall. Pfft!

(CLOETE's imagination is too much for him. He faints, falling with a loud thump. BARRY claps his hands, brings him round.)

Come on now, Cloete, on your feet.

CLOETE: Yirra, James.

BARRY: Yes, I'm sorry Captain. The biggest men have the farthest to fall.

CLOETE: That will make medical history in Cape Town, blerry hell.

BARRY: There'll be a bump. You should see to it.

CLOETE: Look, it's been on my mind, a...friend of mine—

BARRY: I must—

CLOETE: I'll be brief. When younger, my friend was—flighty, as most young men are...

BARRY: A return of the clap is it, Cloete? Drop by the clinic.

CLOETE: I'm talking about a *friend*, Barry, not myself! *(Holding his head.)* Ach, damn it. He's been asked to—watch, if you will, someone—watch him closely and—well, he can't refuse. He is over a barrel. Though my friend seems like a dog with a stick beating its back, he is not. Do you take me?

BARRY: I begin to...follow.

CLOETE: Speak to Struwig. He knows what I'm doing. It will all come out.

BARRY: *(Thoughtfully.)* Get some cool water for that head.

(CLOETE exits. BARRY enters the bedroom.)

LADY MARY: Oh, so red, and wrinkled.

BARRY: How is the pain?

LADY MARY: It is bearable, for such a treasure. I have never been so free, so large and so powerful. This little one, all my own, all the world's, *I* give him life! *(Beat.)* Would you—hold him?

BARRY: You allow me?

LADY MARY: Yes, of course.

BARRY: So much beauty. Little fingers. Tiny head.

LADY MARY: ...Dr. Barry?

BARRY: Can a man not cry?

LADY MARY: I have never known one to do so.

(SOMERSET enters.)

SOMERSET: Give him to his mother, Barry.

LADY MARY: Charles.

SOMERSET: I'm warning you.

LADY MARY: Charles, please!

SOMERSET: Leave us, doctor. Now! Stay away from my family.

Scene Twenty Four Love

>*(DANTZEN and BARRY, in BARRY's rooms.)*

BARRY: I wish you could have been there—that baby, and that woman! Such a strong need to live, to have their life together.

DANTZEN: Your baby—

BARRY: Dantzen…

DANTZEN: —wasn't yours. It was not welcome, not made with joy. That's how they should come when they come. Eh?

BARRY: …What's it like?

DANTZEN: Mm. Full of laughter. Can't stop smiling. Can't stop touching.

BARRY: How did you learn such gentle hands? You should be a doctor, a musician. Any number of things.

DANTZEN: Why can't I be a man with gentle hands.

>*(She laughs. They both laugh, a new sound between them.)*

BARRY: May I?

>*(She takes DANTZEN's hand, looks, touches; then kisses his palm.)*

DANTZEN: I'm not your salvation.

BARRY: Better men than you have been discovered in a stable, Dantzen. So the story goes.

DANTZEN: Not by you, doctor.

BARRY: Call me Marian? My real name.

(She kisses him.)

DANTZEN: You don't know what you're doing.

BARRY: I think at last I do.

DANTZEN: What is it you want from me.

BARRY: Your love.

DANTZEN: Because I'm here?

BARRY: No.

DANTZEN: Just use your tongue and say it.

BARRY: It's not enough. To live with you. To lie alone in separate rooms. I need you. And more.

DANTZEN: We could die for these words.

BARRY: No one can hear us. I want everything that still has the power to shake the universe. I want you.

DANTZEN: Listen to yourself, I want, I want.

BARRY: What do *you* want?

(Pause.)

DANTZEN: …To be here, when the universe is shaken. On this ground.

BARRY: Don't you feel it?

(She kisses him again.)

DANTZEN: You are such a good white man. Terrifyingly good.

(He kisses her.)

So in love with death.

(Then pulls away sharply to listen.)

BARRY: It's nothing.

DANTZEN: Always, always be aware. To stay alive.

(She takes off his shirt.)

BARRY: Say you will.

DANTZEN: Yes, then.

BARRY: Tell me why.

DANTZEN: I lose everything. One generation ago I was free. This is the worst thing I could do to them. This is the warmest thing I can do with you. I desire warmth. Beyond the most imaginative of them.

BARRY: But you don't love me.

DANTZEN: Love is too simple, to say what I feel.

BARRY: Good.

(She takes off her shirt.)

DANTZEN: Marian. Maqoma. *My* real name.

(On his body is a long scar.)

BARRY: Maqoma.... How did you get this?

DANTZEN: The vineyard. My father died that day. Our histories on our bodies, all the world can read; but a body's just the border of a place they will never possess. We are our own maps of the world.

BARRY: You are beautiful. My beautiful friend.

Scene Twenty Five   White Tiger

(SOMERSET's bedchamber. He stands at the window.)

LADY MARY: Come to bed, you're so restless.

SOMERSET: Can't sleep.

LADY MARY: If you feel you'll disturb me, you won't. I am better, so much better. And so thankful. Come to bed now.

(He doesn't. She joins him at the window.)

A beautiful moon.

SOMERSET: There's no moon like the African one. Hot, pure.

LADY MARY: I'm beginning to sense it, its tug on the heart. I begin to love it here. ...Charles?

SOMERSET: You dream of him.

LADY MARY: Dream of...who?

SOMERSET: Dr. Barry. Night after night.

LADY MARY: I'm...not aware of it.

SOMERSET: Why does he pull you?

LADY MARY: I don't dream of him, Charles.

(He moves away.)

He interests me, yes. He is...unlike anyone I've ever encountered. I owe him my life. Charles. I am sorry. But dreams—you are wrong.

(He strokes the tiger hide.)

SOMERSET: There are no tigers in Africa. Did you know that? Just this hide, from my travels. A displaced creature. In India they believe many things of the tiger. It has a soul, it once was human—exiled for bad behaviour. So now it haunts the places of men.

LADY MARY: So sad.

SOMERSET: This was *my* tiger. It came out of nowhere, looked me straight in the eye. It was mine, we both knew it, that tiger and I. Those eyes, God, the eyes. It leapt, I fired—they were gone from the earth. Spirit to spirit, a creature to match me. I want—I will accept—nothing less.

(Pause.)

LADY MARY: Charles.

SOMERSET: Don't hang on me, woman—go to bed. ...Are you hurt?

LADY MARY: No. No.

SOMERSET: I shall send him away—tomorrow, at once!

Scene Twenty Six A Light

(BARRY in a tin tub, washing.)

DANTZEN: ...so he tried to hide, but with no leafy shelter to disappear into, he also was killed. The cat and the forest were safer when they were friends—but they did not know it, yes?

BARRY: Tell me another. The two-faced, with no heart. Tell me that one again.

DANTZEN: This one first. Think about it.

BARRY: Let me wash you.

DANTZEN: Shh.

(A sound, they freeze. DANTZEN goes to the door. LADY SOMERSET is outside.)

DANTZEN: Your Ladyship. *(He bows.)*

LADY MARY: Is Dr. Barry at home?

DANTZEN: The doctor is—indisposed, Your Ladyship.

BARRY: *(Calls.)* I won't be a moment, Lady Somerset.

(She has put on a robe, and now enters.)

LADY MARY: I saw your light, doctor. I very much fear...

BARRY: What is it? Thank you, Dantzen.

(He moves away.)

LADY MARY: I fear I've done you a wrong, unknowingly.

BARRY: Tell me.

LADY MARY: Lord Somerset insists...that you must move on. Oh I feel foolish. I have been dreaming—of you, so he tells me. Though I am not aware of it.

BARRY: Of me?

LADY MARY: He is wrong, of course.

BARRY: Of course.

LADY MARY: This seems to be causing...some friction. Between us. It must be my fault, I have somehow—

BARRY: No. Thank you. You remind me of...priorities. I've grown tired of fighting. I'll go quietly.

LADY MARY: No, really, I—

BARRY: I almost welcome it.

DANTZEN: Captain Cloete, meneer. Is in the hedge.

BARRY: Is he with you?

LADY MARY: I came alone.

DANTZEN: He is certainly hiding, meneer.

BARRY: Ask him to step in.

(DANTZEN goes out. To LADY SOMERSET.)

You love your husband.

LADY MARY: He is wonderful. A good father for my boy. I've never loved before. But I do love this man.

(CLOETE precedes DANTZEN inside.)

CLOETE: Your Ladyship. Forgive me, I saw you crossing the grounds, couldn't help but notice. A lady, alone, at night.

LADY MARY: I...couldn't sleep.

CLOETE: I decided to wait, escort you back to Government House.

LADY MARY: It's not far.

CLOETE: The grounds are dark. At night, one cannot always— there are lions.

BARRY: Your Ladyship. I thank you. And whatever I decide, none of it is your doing.

LADY MARY: We need you in Cape Town.

(LADY SOMERSET exits.)

CLOETE: Mind yourself, Barry. Stay out of his way, for he's going down. Overtaxation, misuse of funds—I've uncovered it all. I've got him now, ja?

(CLOETE exits.)

BARRY: What was he doing there. Somerset going down?

DANTZEN: Your robe.

(He pulls it closed.)

You're taking chances.

BARRY: Yes, I am! I'll let go, a new posting. Start again, start clean. With you. Will you come with me?

DANTZEN: How you love this. You are laughing.

BARRY: I can taste it, life is happening, we are ripping great strips out of it!

DANTZEN: I am with you.

BARRY: Kiss me.

(She kisses him. CLOETE reappears; is staggered by what he sees.)

CLOETE: Lady Mary asked…and the door was ajar…the dark is intense. I had *hoped* for a light.

(He wheels, exits.)

DANTZEN: I am dead.

BARRY: Oh God.

DANTZEN: I'll leave now. Go up country, hide away. I am dead else.

BARRY: Cloete will say nothing, surely.

DANTZEN: Forget we are man and man—even man and woman. This is white skin and black skin. This he will not forget. And *you* may be dead with me. You know I am right.

BARRY: Maqoma.

DANTZEN: In the bush, near the veldt. Where the road turns for the Hemel, there's a place. I will wait there til morning, give you time. Think it through—and let me go.

(DANTZEN runs, pulling off his shirt, to TRACKER's place, crouches, observes the following scene from there—and becomes the TRACKER.)

Scene Twenty Seven   Early Morning

(SOMERSET's room of business, dawn.)

SOMERSET: This had better be good, Captain.

CLOETE: I have news for Your Lordship that will get Barry out of your way with all speed. I have discovered—

(LADY SOMERSET enters.)

SOMERSET: Come man! Don't stand there turned to stone—out with it!

CLOETE: Your Lordship, I—

SOMERSET: Mary, leave us.

LADY MARY: You are speaking of Dr. Barry? Charles, I cannot allow you—

SOMERSET: This is none of your affair.

CLOETE: If I may be bold. Pack him off to some other colony. Mauritius is fighting a cholera outbreak—they need doctors. He *welcomes* danger. *(Glancing at LADY SOMERSET.)* He seduces it, Your Lordship.

SOMERSET: What are you suggesting. Go, Mary.

LADY MARY: I will not. Whatever he's done, whatever you *think* that he's done. He deserves a champion, as you're both so against him.

SOMERSET: So be it. Go ahead, Captain, out with it.

CLOETE: If you're certain. *(Pulls out a letter.)* He is evil, Your Lordship. I—intercepted this, this morning, from Daniel De Groot.

SOMERSET: *(Scanning.)* "...the kaffir boy you are seeking. If you'll pay his passage...and sixty rix dollars...he is yours." Is that it? Don't trifle with me, Captain. There must be something more than this!

CLOETE: Don't you see? It's unspeakable. It's Barry himself.

SOMERSET: What.

CLOETE: He is—intimate...

SOMERSET: Intimate! With whom!

CLOETE: ...with his kaffirs. That is why he is after this boy. And with him he calls Dantzen, there is no doubt. I saw them with my own eyes.

LADY MARY: ...No.

SOMERSET: *(Quiet.)* We must tighten our belts, let go of luxuries, isn't that so?

CLOETE: Yes, Your Excellency.

SOMERSET: But. Do not break the news to him. Let me do that. Let him *go* to Mauritius—if they'll have him.

(BARRY has entered. Pause. LADY SOMERSET goes to BARRY, slaps him, hard. Exits.)

CLOETE: You could hang for what you're doing with that boy!

(CLOETE exits.)

BARRY: I've come to tender my resignation. My life waits for me, near the Hemel. I'll travel, north, into the heart of it, out of your influence. A doctor, on my own terms. At last.

SOMERSET: You have no idea, do you? A wave of chaos on every shore you touch. Good bye, James—or whatever your name is.

BARRY: Governor. You're about to be recalled to England, did Cloete tell you that? He's a hard worker, needs a promotion. I shouldn't be surprised if you're stripped of your title. That will bring me great joy.

SOMERSET: *(A roar.)* Get out of my sight!

Photo by Norma Rodgers

Photo by Andrée Lanthier

Scene Twenty Eight The Dark Continent

> *(1850. The TRACKER simultaneously tells the story and lives his father's through-line.)*

TRACKER: It has come. We are there. It is dawning; my father waits. He did not see it coming. I know now, I know all of it. Sun rising, he waits, my father. In the thorns, for his mlungu.

> *(SOMERSET, again in grinning hunting mask and with a rifle, appears in the veldt. MAGGIE moves through. BARRY enters, and sits, shrunken, old. This is her mightmare, time compressed. The stalking patterns with MAGGIE and SOMERSET continue to the end of the play, while the real scene with GALAWA carries on.)*

SOMERSET: Boy.

TRACKER: The Governor's men. A runaway kaffir.

SOMERSET: I'm glad I found you.

TRACKER: It was simple. They moved quickly. Good trackers.

SOMERSET: I have a job for you.

TRACKER: One man.

SOMERSET: I'm looking for a pest. He's been into my stable, defiled it.

TRACKER: One bullet.

SOMERSET: *(He raises the rifle.)* I'm following you.

TRACKER: These tracks are fresh, blood not yet congealed.

SOMERSET: Yes, very fresh.

TRACKER: This is the blood of a man, not a beast.

SOMERSET: No. It's the blood of a beast.

(SOMERSET cocks the rifle.)

TRACKER: He said, my father: At least look me in the eye when you do it.

(SOMERSET shoots. All movements cease as shots are fired. The sound reverberates, wild animals shriek and roar. BARRY relives this moment again and again.)

BARRY: NO!!!

TRACKER: The foot fits the footprint, the last piece in place. Two years ago, emancipation. Anonymous money frees me, and I suspect, start the journey back. I am here, he is here—after postings, promotions that once he desired, all over the globe—come back at the end to the Hemel and Aarde. Where the road turned. Forever. *(Beat.)* Turn around, doctor.

(BARRY turns.)

BARRY: Where did you come from?

TRACKER: I'm a tracker.

BARRY: I'm ill, I don't know you.

TRACKER: The brothers told me your story, that you've come here to die. Do you know they talk behind your back?

BARRY: They are human. It is normal.

TRACKER: Is this normal—you send a small fortune to a kaffir you never met.

BARRY: ...Galawa.

TRACKER: It's taken a long time. But I'd find you one day, so I swore.

(SOMERSET fires. BARRY remembers.)

60 rix dollars, and the cost of my passage. Instead,

silence. I slowly forgot. Grew into my life, tracking in Nepal. Why were you silent with me?

(CLOETE appears, above, watches SOMERSET.)

BARRY: An old duelling partner, fat and happy, rediscovers a letter. I'd never received it. His revulsion's worn off, memories of old times remain.

CLOETE: Beware the hungry dog, ja? It finds its meal.

(SOMERSET raises his rifle at CLOETE, who disappears. SOMERSET fires, BARRY remembers.)

BARRY: He sent me the letter. I was ailing, in Canada, dying of cold. I wrote the maharajah. And you received the money. A stab in the dark, on my part. Hit its mark.

(African dusk grows; MAGGIE crosses BARRY's path; BARRY watches her.)

Hit its mark.

TRACKER: Say it, doctor.

BARRY: I was a woman.

TRACKER: This I know.

BARRY: I loved your father.

(SOMERSET fires. BARRY remembers.)

And I killed him.

TRACKER: Mlungu, I've spent a lifetime conquering my fear of you.

(Pause.)

BARRY: Tell me a story, Galawa. Your father's. The Two-Faced.

TRACKER: In the grasses, we are walking. "Don't fear them, Galawa", he says. "If you do, you'll be trapped, you will never get free." When I track tigers, mlungu, I remember his words. We are loners together, those tigers and I, refusing to be frightened.

BARRY: Yes.

A woman enters a forest where the Two-Faced lives. She is on her own business, and she is afraid. He pounces, she escapes with her life, but her skin is now dappled like the skin he wears. She is become light and shadow, good and evil. Two eyes grow in the back of her head. Her people shun her, but pay for her knowledge. It is knowledge they don't want to carry themselves. She is lonely, unusual, returns to the forest. She wants this Two-Faced to know of her burden. She sees him, he sees her, and this time is different—she is full of joy! Then he jumps up and grabs her—by the back of the neck—and breaks it—*(Snap sound with his tongue.)*, like that!

(The TRACKER says the lines in Xhosa, then repeats them in English:)

Sel waquondiswa nge thamsanqa—And the one face says, "did you never know what was luck?" *Waqeqeshwa nangobuqhawe boqobo?*—The other face says, "and what was real courage?"

(They observe each other.)

BARRY: I had a dream...of the future. I see him over, and over, and over.

TRACKER: *Xa uqabela ingwe, mlungu, uyiqabela unom'phelo.* When you ride the tiger, white man, you ride it forever.

(SOMERSET fires; the tiger roars.

The End.)

The Tracker

- Cap-Saint-Ignace
- Sainte-Marie (Beauce)
Québec, Canada
1996